Larry Ukali
Johnson-Redd

PART 2 ALSO
AVAILABLE

American
Challenges
In The
Obama
Era Part 1

American Challenges In The Obama Era Part 1
Copyright © 2025 by Larry Ukali Johnson-Redd

ISBN: 979-8894792071 (sc)
ISBN: 979-8894792088 (e)

The Reading Glass
BOOKS

The Reading Glass Books
(888) 420-3050
www.readingglassbooks.com
fulfillment@readingglassbooks.com

AMERICAN CHALLENGES IN THE OBAMA ERA Part 1

This book is dedicated to all open minded people who understand we will not always agree about every idea or poem but we should we should be willing to read, write and discuss everything By its title American Challenges in the Obama Era is both full of inside the box and outside the box thinking. Comprehensive thinking and discussions of various ideas and poems should be encouraged and not discouraged.

I hope you will read this book and respond to me on my facebook page using my name on facebook to locate my page. I also hope you will visit me on You Tube and read my other books. I am publishing Long Distance Love for the first time a kindle Book at the same time I am publishing this book American Challenges In The Obama Era. I am also publishing. Long Distance Love is a memoir of my 2005 trip to Nigeria that included a courtship with a young Nigerian woman as well as a memorable set of experiences during my 10-day stay in Nigeria, West Africa.

My first book Journey To The Motherland, From San Francisco to Benin City is also available as a paperback book on my Journey Books Page at Amazon.com. for $5.00 plus shipping. The link is: http://www.amazon.com/Journey-Motherland-Francisco-Benin- City/ dp/0967422639/ref=nosim/?tag=chickenajourn-20

Journey Books is my book distribution company.

My beloved book History To Destiny Through Afrocentric Poetry continues to be out of print however I have made History To Destiny a Kindle e-book and I hope you will read the new and old spoken word style poetry in more than 300 pages .History To Destiny like all my e-books costs $.99 cents each.

Dedication

This book American Challenges In The Obama Era part 1 is dedicated to my beautiful immediate, nuclear and extended family. This book is also dedicated to those who feel governments should help people and not kill people with excessive deadly police or armed force.

Finally this book is dedicated to the Oscar Grant and his family especially his mom and daughter. We all are potentially Oscar Grant! The family of the late Oscar Grant deserves all of our support as they seek justice for the late Oscar Grant.

Lastly this book is dedicated to all people who realize we all have to work together- better to make the world a better place for us all by prioritizing the most in need! I also am dedicating this book to Floyd B., Ahmad Alvin Mayberry and family, Rudolph Lewis and his family and Itibari M. Zulu, Wanda Sabir and the Rawsisters.com organization for their friendship, support , understanding and reviews.

Larry Ukali Johnson-Redd- Revised 2013: Biography

Larry Ukali Johnson-Redd, born 1952 in San Francisco, graduated from Balboa High School in 1970 and entered University of San Francisco and received a B.A. in 1974 in Political Science and Ethnic Studies (African American). His quest for education continued at Golden Gate University in San Francisco where he received a Masters in Public Administration 1976 (MPA). In 2004 Ukali earned his Masters of Arts in Educational Administration and his Administrative Credential!

Ukali's books and Black Love Spoken Word:
The Black Expatriate in Africa (1982)
Journey to the Motherland, From San Francisco to Benin City-
   Autobiographical Novel (2002)
History To Destiny Through Afrocentric Poetry (2004)
Loving Black Women: Essays and Spoken Word (2006)
New book: 2010-Long Distance Love
Ukali has delivered his unique Black Love Spoken Word from Sacramento to L. A. to San Francisco to Brooklyn NY! I would love to be invited to your area, program or event as a lecturer, poet or panelist or any combination!

http://www.youtube.com/user/ukalitheafrican
http://www.blackplanet.com/your_page/videos/index.html? profile_id=39945499&profile_name=Ukal2003&user_id=39945499&usernam
http://www.youtube.com/watch?v=uPz7xAnLF9M
http://www.nathanielturner.com/larryuklaijohnsonreddtable.htm

Larry Ukali Johnson-Redd- (A Memoir)! Ukali has completed American Challenges in the Obama Era Part 1 and Long Distance Love. In 2013 Ukali is currently working on American Challenges In the Obama Part 2.

In April 2010 Ukali participated in the SF Kings of Poetry-A DVD will soon be released! Larry can be contacted at 415-425-6711 or **mailto:ljredd52@aol.com**

Table of Contents

From President-Elect To President Barack Obama

Congratulations are still in order for President Barack Obama, the first African-American President in American history! We are into the 70th day of the Barack Obama Presidency and on the ground not much have changed although some African-American men feel some blowback! Blowback of those people who were dead set against a Barack Obama the forward thinking, fair-minded and those who decided to join a coalition to unhitch from the old era of America's past defeated past which included those who said Segregation yesterday, today and Segregation tomorrow!

Most African-Americans remain very proud of President Barack Obama; proud of the stimulus plan he fought hard for and finally was approved! And most of us African-Americans understand that getting a government up and running takes time and implementing needed solutions cannot occur overnight! And the way President Barack Obama came into office he had to clean up some dirty matters left by his predecessors like Bush and Chaney including torture, Quantanamo and the foreign policy reviews that I hope are still on going! So in that thought I am like most African-Americans and I think there are a lot of Americans who may hold that same opinion!

However there are those who cannot wait much longer for positive changes. They have already been layed off! They have already applied for unemployment. They have been unemployed so long they cannot remember their last job. Some have even given up on looking for a job! Some are totally discouraged. They may have worked for Ford, GM and Chrysler! Those whose job continues to be somewhat secure or secure will say the new president should be allowed more time and probably be more understanding but if you are feeling the crunch then you want to see the fastest implementations of stimulus and change as soon as possible all across America!

The policy review on Afghanistan and the rest of the Middle East must continue while Hopefully a break with the Bush war policy against Afghanistan is made to bring peace to Afghanistan without killing its entire people! And clearly resolving the Middle East dilemma of the Palestinians and seeing the establishment must be a foreign policy priority! Africa too must be engaged and new thinking evaluated so that America moves from being chained to its slave past and its past of ugly American intervention first by looking at it's troubled past in a realistic way and then repairing the past while stepping into a new future! Although many African-American observers may view the Barack Obama presidency as mostly symbolic, Barack Obama still has the chance to be a great American President and a great president for African-America all at the same time! . But on the70th day of the Barack Obama Presidency, it is clear that the clock is ticking!

Challenges include dismantling the American prison Industrials Complex that expands daily by incarcerating young African-Americans and youth of all cultures in an alarming rate and giving hope to those who have given up and who are in need of stimulus! The failing banks and corporations have been heard and taken good care of to date; now the needs of the rest of us must begin to visibly rise up on the priority list!

President-Elect Barrack Obama and the African-Americans

http://www.conversations-of-africa.yomn.net/

The election is finally over and now that Barack Obama has won and we are feeling good to see an African-American family preparing to move into the White House.

However good we African-Americans and by extension to some extent all Americans feel about our Brother President-Elect Barack Obama, we African-Americans are being whipped and spanked with joblessness, unemployment, underemployment, losing mortgages and housing, becoming homeless and hitting the bottom of the barrel. Yet we witness the collapse of GM, and the auto industry, desperation, the collapsing financial industry lined up to get billions of Government tax funds as a stimulus to resuscitate these ailing industries.

George Bush threw America head long into 2 wars in Iraq and Afghanistan that stimulated weapon making industries and a few favored no bid contractors like Halliburton Corporation however the American economy tanked right as the presidential election was ending exposing the bankruptcy of the Bush Administration and Bush years to the American public!

The weight of war and the billions sent every month to Iraq and Afghanistan have been great factors in bankrupting the American economy however African-Americans were the first victims of Bush neglect because African-American interests were invisible to George W. Bush.

We African-Americans were the first to feel the Bush neglect suffering all 8 years including the well-known neglect of Katrina storm/flood victims. Yet we African-Americans should not have been ignored because we are like the canaries in a coal mine. Minors carry Canaries into the mines because these birds will be the first to sound an alarm about air quality. In the same way if African-Americans are doing okay economically one could say every one else is also doing wel l. George Bush had such blinders on that he could not see, feel or hear the cries of anguish in our communities,until Wall Street and Main Street started crumbling threatening all of America. We felt the Bush neglect and now we need to have our needs met too!

Now billions are being distributed to millionaire and billionaire companies and banks while African-Americans and other rural and urban poor are waiting at the back of the line. And we are at the back of the line waiting for help to trickle down needing jobs and paid job-training programs in our communities to be greatly expanded to employ the urban millions of unemployed. President Elect Barack Obama please do not leave us at the back of the line behind the banks, financial industries and auto companies waiting for help to trickle down! I know you are not yet President however please send a signal with your magnificent communication skills that you get it because we all realize that George W. Bush will never get it

The African-American economic needs are on the scale addressed by the WPA of the mid 1930's and1940's! Addressing African-American and urban poor economic needs will require a Civilian Job Corps for those24 years and older to receive training for old and new economy jobs, along with dramatic expansion of Job Corps Centers for high-risk youth 16 to 24 years old to meet growing economic and job training needs. Community based organizations that manage non-profit job training programs will also need to be dramatically expanded even larger than the Concentrated Employment and Training Programs of the past.

African-Americans like all other Americans are waiting for Barack Obama to turn things around for the middle class but also for the working class and the under classes where we African-Americans are well represented! We are also well represented among those with adjustable rate loans!

We African-Americans join with all other Americans in wishing President-Elect Barack Obama success in his efforts to resuscitate America including African-Americans. We African-Americans also need stimulus funds all over this country as soon as possible more than the failed bankers, failing Insurance Companies and failing automakers!

President-Elect Barack Obama And The World

The New American President-Elect will become the first openly African-American President when he is inaugurated Jan 20, 2009 in American history!

This presidency while widely supported among all populations in the USA will be viewed historically by African-Americans as a step away from the chattel slavery this country was founded on in contradiction of it's stated ideals and a step closer to an era of real liberation! The only way to make it a real break is to clean house on the dirty past and then move forward!!

The dawning of a new era offers a chance to rethink and redesign American Foreign Policy interests and objectives! The question arises immediately if Obama will continue to push for change having now won the Presidency or settle for the more of the same foreign policy!

If Obama is going to rethink US Foreign Policy interests and objectives then and only then could critical reviews and decisions that need to be made about the USA continuing to act as the world policeman and ugly American could be made!

Currently American Foreign Policy interests revolve around making sure American capitalists can ruthlessly exploit all markets in every part of the world or changing and or replacing any regime that chooses a different type of government than the US Government or a Government that is not totally considered a pro-American Government like Cuba or Venezuela!

In order to totally shed the image of the ugly American interventionist or world policeman image Obama must end the US occupations of Iraq first and to also withdraw from Afghanistan as soon as possible!

To change USA Foreign Policy objectives and interests, the Obama Administration must once again raise Human Rights to the top of the Foreign and Domestic Policy Agenda thus redesigning American foreign policy interests and objectives!

Promoting change as a candidate is easier than actually implementing a changing of political and or economic objectives and interests and selling those changes to the American people however under an Obama Administration owes it to the American people to launch comprehensive Congressional and Administration investigations of torture in the domestic area including investigation of allegations of torture of the San Francisco 8 (some former Black Panthers) and the Angola 3 political prisoners as well as other Counter Intelligence Program era African-American political prisoner as who were victimized by dirty tricks of the government domestically as well as launching a comprehensive investigation of Bush Administration torture in Iraq, Quantanamo, Cuba and many other countries that the USA used to carry out torture. A constitutional democracy like the USA should never be involved in torture of Americans, African-Americans and not against any people defending their country or people so it will not happen to Americans abroad!

Once torture is studied in depth the American people can better understand how Bush acted as a rogue bully of a world policeman and then these political prisoners must be freed! These investigations should be modeled on the South African Truth Commissions and at the conclusion some of these political prisoners like the Angola 3, Mumia Abdul Jamal and the San Francisco 8 should be released. Then the USA can denounce torture as an instrument of state policy once and for all and the world will give the USA a brand new start in world affairs. Death by lynching and Tazer shot deaths should also be included in these new Truth Commissions investigations so America could apologize and come clean.

These moves would show a course being chartered away from the Ugly American rightwing regime changing intervention being committed against countries that may disagree with US policies or interests as well as make a complete break with the dirty tricks and dirty war launched against African-American dissidents and political prisoners from the past to the present like Troy Davis.. These completed investigations will also provide a basis for lifting the economic blockade of Cuba.

I also propose an African Commission be established to support of and /or implement a United States of Africa or Federated State of Africa if Africans on the continent embrace this dynamic concept. This is a time for thinking out of the box.

Obama and the Concept of a United States of Africa

The concept of the United States of Africa or some form of democratically selected Federated African Continent-Wide State is that Africa needs to stand up on it's own as a united continent and government as soon as a United States of Africa or a Federated African State it can be implemented democratically by the people who live on the African Continent!

If a Federated State of Africa can emerge, then the need for regional wars in Congo, Sudan, and Somalia will slowly but surely disappear in a united Africa.

Africa as a united government and country would not need foreign assistance to feed, clothe, house, employ and develop its people and resources. President-Elect Obama has to learn many new concepts, budgets and policies however Obama also needs to learn more about the concept of a United States of Africa!

I congratulate President–Elect Barack Obama and his beautiful family for winning a tough election as they prepare to move into the White House!

Sincerely,

Larry Ukali Johnson-Redd

Announcement Checkout Conversations of Africa

From Juneteeth to Barack Obama: Rethinking Black Liberation This interview occurred in Jan.2009!

My guest this week on Conversations of Africa will be Rudolph Lewis, Editor of Chicken Bones an On-Line Magazine dedicated to promoting African-American and African Literature and Thought! We will discuss Black Liberation issues from yesterdays gone by to the contemporary scene we experience today including the change if any we have experienced so far from the election of President Barack Obama!

Rudolph wrote a must read piece during African-American history Month titled:

What *Black Liberation means in the Obama Era* where he speaks to a series of concerns for the disconnectedness between African-Americans mainly youth and elders who experienced segregation directly during the 50's and sixties and contemporary African-American youth who experience the continuing ills of American society like police brutality /prison guard brutality and economic underdevelopment without being able to connect the dots and see the need to work together with and respect older generation folks to regenerate the cultural steam needed for progress and unity inside of an economic crisis plagued America!

How do we define Black Liberation in these bizarre situations we find ourselves in the dawning age of Obama?

Obamaland

Obama land
In America
Your dad hails
From Kenya Africa

Obama
A more perfect union
Obama stand for
All women and men

Obama
Save us from the Tazer
Obama
While handcuffed
9 times is too much

Obama
Give us our rights
As you run for the Blacks
And you run for the whites

Obama
Your day
has come
Obama#1

Obama
We will vote
For you
Percentage 92

Obama restore
All human rights
As President
Of Blacks, Browns, Red Yellow and Whites

As we enter
The voter's booths
Our ancestors with us
With truth and soul our root

Obama
do your best
to help out all
of us we trust

Obama help the
home less in the inner city
Obama help Africa
See the power of Unity

Obama support
all in America
Obama support
The United States of Africa

Obama empower
us all
On Malcolm and Martin's
Shoulders stand tall

Stand up
for all of America
Obama our ancestor's call
Obama for us all

Peace and freedom
in Obama Land
Stand and win
In America and Africa

Obama unite and free
The American land
Free the people of
Obamaland

JOBS, JOBS AND MORE JOBS NEEDED AS SOON AS POSSIBLE ALL OVER THE USA:

Stimulus ll, A Stimulus For The People of the USA Revised!
My advice to President Barack Obama By Larry Johnson-Redd Part 1

There is a need for Jobs, Jobs and more Jobs! We need a JOB Training, JOB Creation and JOB Placement Program that pays at least a living wage to job seekers and completes the training with Job Placement in a mega sized effort for those most in need to heal the job losses! Other than a massive effort of this type Obama may be a meaningless or only symbolic 1 term President! Despite what is being said about a jobless recovery this still remains a depression if you lost your job or had your hours cut or lost your home, housing or health care as millions have! It may be only a recession only if it was other people who lost their jobs, homes, and health insurance!

There is so much selfishness expressed by tea baggers and others who have spoken out against the new and old have-nots and the pressing need for jobs and health care needs!! Who will stand up to fed, clothe, house and employ the millions of unemployed, the private sector alone? And yet those who oppose helping those in need fall woefully silent of budgetary screams when the cost of sending thousands more to intervene in other countries is brought up wrapping themselves in outright hypocrisy! The cost of war and nation building abroad far exceeds the cost of helping those most in need locally especially when 45,000 per year die from a lack of heath care access in the richest country in the world with one of the best medical care systems in the world!

Who would have thought with the suffering of 45,000 people dieing preventable deaths per year that getting health care in place for those who do not have it would be so difficult! And how can this great feat be done with out the public option. Speaker Pelosi and House Democrats have and are continuing the fight! Across the country this month 20,000 more jobs have been lost in Jan/ Feb 2010!

Since the matter is still pending efforts should be made to push up implementation so that all Americans can get affordable health care and jobs. It doesn't matter if you are in earthquake-ravaged Haiti! The people of our beloved Haiti deserve all the help that they are getting and so too do the people of the USA deserve help at least equal to the help received by Wall Street! In my original Stimulus ll Proposal there should have been 50 to 100 Billion allocated to a special fund to rewrite affordable mortgages for underwater homeowners who have suffered from the practices of an under regulated Wall Street. These funds should be spent right away to keep people who still have a chance to stay in their homes and rescued from the underwater status where their newly devalued houses are worth less than the value of the highly priced and exploitative mortgages!

Underwater recovery funds will help the housing industry recover as well! The Banks have failed the people and the main populous issue of the tea party would suddenly be a non-issue and the hurting pain would be eased in the USA!

Then you look at MSNBC sponsored free health clinics all over the country and people flocking by the thousands to free clinics all over the USA and you wonder why so many who have Medicare or Private health care insurance along with the greedy health insurance industry are blocking inclusion of those suffering 45 Thousand preventable deaths! And the continuing heath care discrepancy where African-Americans live 5 to10 years shorter than other Americans is unacceptable but un-addressed in the USA! Why?

The Stimulus l is beginning to get middle class people back to work but the trickledown is not helping the people who are obviously not middle class and so that is why we need the focused help out limned in my Stimulus ll proposal! Stimulus1 and Stimulus ll together will stimulate America and its economy from the bottom up and from the top down! If aspects of my original Stimulus ll proposal are implemented nationally like the National Adult Job Corps for workers 25 to 65 or even Obama's new proposed Jobs Bill are implemented then the effort cold lower the unemployment rate nationally to 5 to

6% or even lower then the country will be will be stimulated from the grassroots Obama supporters up or from the ground up instead of the bail out of the super rich only! Finally America and the others are to be congratulated for the rescue of Haiti devastated by the great earthquake 6 miles from the surface of the earth! Now is the time the rescue of America must be completed with that same sense of urgency after the 8 years of devastation of the lower economic classes by the George Bush Administration and the mismanagement from Wall Street to the auto industry! Wall Street is back on its feet and the Automobile Industry has been rescued! Now is the time to rescue the American People!

My Original Stimulus ll Proposal Part 2

The mega sized Finance, Banking and Insurance Sector including Wall Street of the US Economy have had their stimulus from the TARP and other government interventions and so has the Car Industry! This was taxpayer money to be paid back! Now many of them would like to pay out big bonuses to top executives at the end of this year without paying back all of more than 1 trillion dollars plus any interest owed! Now there is a 10.2% overall unemployment rate that means 15 to 30% unemployment rate among African-Americans! Something dramatic must be done to turn this horrible jobless recovery into a job creation and job expansion recovery or the President and his party will not have enough supporters to keep a friendly Congress!

I advise President Obama to collect the 1 Trillion Dollars and any interest back as soon as possible from those recipients who owe before 1 mega bonus is given out.

I advise that the 1 trillion be spent to help fund Stimulus ll aimed at the states and Washington DC, like California and the other states with deficits, small business grants to hire Stimulus ll implementation workers and the creation of a National Adult Job Corps for those who want to work aged from 25 to 65 including the unemployed, underemployed (Part timers who want full time work and homeless people who want to work and live in apartments or other housing)!

The States and Washington D.C. Share 200 Billion Dollars Of the 1 Trillion dollars recovered, 200 billion should be given to the states, first to states with deficits like California and then to all states including the District of Columbia that has more people than many small states should share equally whatever is left of the 200 Billion to hire staff of all levels!

The National Adult Job Training Corps should be funded with 400 Billion Dollars.

The National Adult Job Corps for those who want to work aged from 25 to 65 including the unemployed, underemployed (Part timers who want full time work and homeless people who want to work)! This NAJC would be like CETA of the Clinton Years and the WPA of the forties and thirties during similar depressed times. This would be the people's stimulus with stipend paying job training, job preparation and job placement services. Although the Dept. of Labor and Housing and Urban Development could administer these funds, services will be contracted out to Non-Profit Organizations, including green jobs outfits, social service corporations and cities / states where appropriate!

Small Businesses should be given *300 Billion 45% in grants and 45 % loans and 10 % to Business Incubator Centers, Green Job Developers and Small Business Start Ups! * Here is where 100 billion could be utilized for underwater homeowners to finance affordable re financing! This is a change from my original proposal!

This part of Stimulus ll or the People's Stimulus of *300 Billion exclusively for new hires to assist the effort to implement the recovery of small businesses and implement Stimulus ll for 1 year on a basis of 45 % of the new hires coming from general applicants and 45% of new hires could be mandated to be NAJC graduates as full time employees! The SBA could also be directed to give small businesses additional loans at say 3% from existing SBA funds. The 10 % remaining in this part of the Stimulus ll could be given as grants to small business incubator centers, Green Job Builders and small business start-ups on a competitive basis! Again there are many non-profits ready to compete for these contracts. The refinancing out of this special 100 billion dollar fund would end the bleeding and restore a huge number of homeowners who remain at risk of foreclosure!

Conclusion

I advise President Obama to implement Stimulus ll and claim his spot in history stimulating the recovery of the US Economy and relieve the heavy economic pressure on the Obama supporters in many cases who are the most in need of a hand up in this time of suffering by the lower levels of American Society. Nation building like charity begins locally- at home. Stimulus ll could help turn things around and be the difference in second term prospects and winning in 2010 by mobilizing the base! Momentum for Stimulus ll could also receive a boost and be the next priority or second step to winning the health care overhaul legislation with a robust public option! If not $400 Billion or $1 trillion President Obama then propose some significant figure and go to work on it!

Stimulus 1 and Stimulus ll will be needed together to speed up the recovery before the crucial November 2010 Congressional Elections if Obama and his supporters move quickly!

Byline

Larry Johnson-Redd is an author of 3 books, Journey to the Motherland, From San Francisco to Benin City available from Amazon.com, History To Destiny-currently out of print and Loving Black Women available at Amazon.com! Larry needs a new literary agent to present his new book "Long Distance Love" a probable international bestseller to publishers! His email is mailto:ljredd52@aol.com also what do you think about a Stimulus ll?

Moving Towards A Strategic National Black Consensus

Moving towards a Strategic National Black Consensus as a framework for working together to improve our Economic, Academic, Cultural, Social and Political Interests. In short the more we move towards a positive mentality upgrade represented by moving towards a Strategic National Black Consensus, the more we internally empower ourselves to achieve our primary, secondary and tertiary political, social, academic cultural economic and political goals the more we will make progress toward liberating ourselves from oppression, depression, self destruction, white supremacy,Black on Black brutality and ultimately Black on Black killing. Study African-American History from Black Inventors to Black victims of lynching, 40 Acres and mule-Reparations to the difference between5/5ths and 3/5ths of a human being in the American constitution and know it!

Why is a consensus among the Blacks in the USA a necessity? In times past African-Americans depended wholly on leaders, however, the best way forward is for African-Americans to respect leaders and but also add more personal energy to resolve issues like the increasingly high incarceration rate, police brutality and other problems of African-American's and the Black on Black murder rate that we observe to be on the increase. This elevation of Black self hate resulting in an increasing number of deaths of primarily young Black men, our future! For the potential of our young Black men's future that are failing school or being failed in greater numbers, we need to come to a broad consensus to accomplish several goals! We must also step up our efforts to educate our minds and learn to know better who our people are: African People all over the world. Reading this whole book is a great step forward in that positive direction of educating our mind!

The first or primary goal is to collectively say to young Black men - boys and young black women - girls, that we support you and want you to have every opportunity necessary to achieve success in school, and job or professional life or college/University!

The secondary goal of any broadly based nationally based strategic consensus must be to communicate to African-American jobless that we as a people prioritize their receiving job training, education, relevant education as well as a paying job for this most important segment of our population to put as many as possible back on a positive career path and paying jobs. Our tertiary or third broad goal must be to assist our people in the greatest numbers possible to avoid street fights and street wars among African-Americans primarily but also between African-Americans and other ethnic or racial groups so we can harness all of our energy for self improvement and self empowerment activities!

The last and most potent reason for a strategic National Black Consensus is to focus our population and the society in general on why reparations must be paid by the US Government to compensate for 400 years of slavery and oppression including the 3/5ths clause of the US Constitution.

In order to press in the most effective way for reparations, we must achieve a consensus of ideas, priorities and goals so we can move forward rapidly to achieve at levels of success a growing majority of our people can support.

Strategic National and International
Consensus among African People in the World

A Consensus of thought for African People all over the world is the first step from inappropriate powerlessness to appropriate empowerment.

Developing the United Black Empowerment Model on a worldwide basis should not have to be stated, however, in this our African World full of scattered Black Nations and Black/African populations, we should all begin to embrace development of an international consensus to eliminate Black on Black murder of all types all over the world.

In the book 'Loving Black Women', I made a call for on All African People's Congress to begin a World Wide African Conversation.

Even though it has not yet happened on a scale envisioned this type of gathering continues to be vital and necessary as black kill other Blacks in Africa, America and in other areas while those with this broadly based thought of an International Strategic Black Consensus to halt acts of Black on Black violence and murder and focus our energies on working together and trading together to develop people to people social, economic, cultural, political and blood ties among our people!

Once we achieve upgraded relationships in our local arenas among ourselves, we will be able to see the importance of the international component of our strategic International and National Black Consensus to assist our people in developing conscious more united outlook and a more united mentality or way of thinking to reduce the negativity of Black on Black self hate and Black on Black killing in all areas where we live in this world.

Once we have developed this united mentality and way of thinking, we will see the emergence of a United States of Africa, African People's Republic or other United African State or Entity. The full expression of an international Black Strategic Consensus would be the convening of a fully representative All African People's Congress made up of Africans from all over the world in Lagos, Nigeria or Accra Ghana outlined in more detail in my book Loving Black Women within an essay titled African World African Identity at the beginning of the book.

African-Americans Mexicans and Other Latios/Latinas

All of the groups listed above include Black skinned people - among the Mexicans and other Latinos/Laminas are many Afro Mexicans in areas like Vera Cruz, Mexico, Honduras, Nicaragua, Brazil, Uruguay, Paraguay, Cuba and throughout the Spanish/Portuguese speaking world.

In the USA, these groups are often manipulated against each other particularly African Americans Mexicans and non gambling Native Americans. The manipulation only benefits white supremacy that harms us all!

The challenge these two populations face so heavily represented at the bottom of this society is for these two less empowered populations to see their political interests are best served by developing cooperation on a consensus of ideas and united practices of those developed ideas in the schools, communities, in the US Congress, and in the general US and Western Hemisphere as a whole!

We must note that in addition to the role Mexico plays hosting African populations of the Afro Mexicans, the US African-American slaves often escaped into Mexico and at that time freedom. When both of these oppressed populations see their common political interests the petty conflicts will end and the united action will proceed.

Ethnic Glue Among African-Americans

My main focus for writing this book is to generate new ideas on developing more Ethnic Glue for African-Americans who may be losing all Ethnic glue as we see more and more Black on Black violence and murder in our communities in the USA.

Still we also see the racism that produced the Jena 6 and the white oppression within the case of the SF-8 many of who are now freed from unjust charges! We also see the 50 bullets fired into innocent until proven guilty late Sean Bell in New York City. We see the rape assault and kidnapping of a Black Sister in West Virginia and other acts of white oppression in a white supremacy State in America.

Still with all of the white on Black and Black on Black violence can we maintain our ethnic glue as African-Americans? Ethnic glue and self-love are one and the same for African-Americans or Africans born in America and African People around the world.

We can but only if we consciously and purposely decide that we as a people will maintain our sense of ethnic glue and self love as a people.

We have to decide anew and again that we will keep our love for each other as a people in special part of our hearts and utilize that love-self love and love of our people as a motivation to end the Black on Black murder and violence that is on the rise among our people especially inside our communities.

We as a people must embrace our humanity as African-Americans and African People in America to show love for each other as a practice instead of self hate or we will make the term ethnic glue a useless term! African- American adults, children and youth should love each other, Africa and Africans with that special love!

We African-Americans have definite African Roots. This was really obvious to me when I lived in Nigeria West Africa for 4 years seeing African Men, African Women as well as African youth and children who looked just like us, identical to all types of African-Americans. However, sharing African roots with Africans and Africa leaves us in a zone of self-hate when we say we love only our American heritage and hate our African heritage. In that zone of self-hate we nurture anti Black sentiments that allow us to proceed down a path of a self-destruction!

Therefore, we must encourage our youth and young people to love Africa and Africans as a part of us African-Americans loving ourselves. We have to love our African self at least as much as we love our American selves as African-Americans to be balanced self-loving African People positively connected to other Africans all over the world and to be our whole self.

In a land disunited and dominated by white supremacy minded people symbolized by George Bush and the other neocons—Neo Conservatives who like the ones proceeding see America as wealth building and Empire Building while being at war with any plan or program that promises to assist African- Americans. These people would also be against African-Americans receiving just and proper reparations of $1,000.00 to $500,000.00 for the middle passage and the 400 plus years of slavery and oppression.

In a land dominated by white supremacy where African-Americans are a minority although a substantial Black Nation, it may be a path to ignore one's own identity while over embracing the majority culture that is guided by white supremacy involving Willie Lynch style divide and conquer tactics to be deployed on African-Americans especially if they/we speak out about our many issues. But can we calculate the costs of ignoring our identity to our people as a whole? We have the power to control our image once we realize how important it is for us to get along with each other better to empower each other.

Continuing the move towards
a Strategic National Black Consensus.

We have to visualize ourselves as African-Americans in a multi-cultural world represented by populations from all over the world. We should practice tolerance and benefit from tolerance in equal measure!

However, we must embrace as many of us as possible a path to peace, progress, development, self improvement and unity or choose to continue down a path that includes Black on Black murder and crime, self-destruction, joblessness and a lack of self-improvement.

Between these two paths, we must individually consciously and hopefully collectively make the choice that will result in our people making as much progress as it is possible to make it in the white supremacy state until we are given justified reparations!

Remember our tax dollars paid for Japanese reparations - given to Japanese who are taken to concentration camps during World War II a few years. These wrongs must be made right!

Until that time comes, we cannot allow ourselves to move towards self- destruction when the path to enhance our chances for success through a strategic national black consensus remains open to us a people. Please make the right decision my people?

Continuing the call for 8th and 9th African People's Congresses and Defining needed African-American preparations!

So we need to and I continue to make the call to have the 8th and 9th All African People's Congresses to empower our powerless people all over the world. We can go home thinking in and out of the box about ways to make progress

However, on an individual basis, we as a people need to rebuild empowerment and embrace self love, ethnic glue, Black Unity, African Awareness more Black self love, less Black self hate until we embrace the path toward a strategic National Black Consensus including a more United State of mind and United Mentality so we can end Black on Black murder and violence and empower ourselves better! Once we are better to ourselves, we will find it easier to define our relationships with other groups, no matter their ethnicity. However self love like charity must begin at home!

The Importance of Africa
to Africans in America or African-Americans

The importance of Africa is central to understanding the heart and soul of African-Americans or more properly Africans in America.

African-Americans live in highly technical modern environment and have no trouble mastering the ways of this society when given a fair chance to use the technology and see it's benefits. However, Africans in America like our African brothers and sisters in Africa have been overwhelmed with the white beauty standards promoted all over the west. And, to many of us here and even to a leaser extent our homeland brothers and sisters have similar ways of looking at shades of Black in terms of white western beauty standards. As a result of such thinking there are many Africans in America who use skin lighteners to even their tone or even lighten their tone. African-Americans or Africans anywhere else who use skin lighteners should wise up and stop this crazy behavior that supports white supremacy.

Those of us who are victims of white supremacy should not glorify our oppressors by trying to bleach skin to make it closer to white skin.

Hopefully, the majority of Africans all over the world from West Papua and New Guinea to Fuji to Africa to the Caribbean/South America region to North America can appreciate all of the shades of Black that we are as African People produce naturally all shades of Black and no one should prefer or favor one shade of black over another. Peter Tosh the late great Jamaican Reggae singer got it right with his song 'If you are a Black Man, You are an African. African People all over the world naturally produce all shades of Black. And of greatest importance to us is the fact that Africa is the homeland of all Africans all over the world.

We have to value our natural African selves as we were made in all of the beautiful shades of Black that we are. We have to appreciate the natural hair, facial shade, color and features. We must love ourselves consciously never favor any shade of Black that appears to be closer to white skin as the only beautiful African skin. All shades of Black are beautiful. As a people we do need to elevate our self-esteem.

However, when I traveled throughout the various regions of Nigeria (1977 to 1981) it was very obvious to me that each region of Nigeria produced Africans, Nigerians of every shade of black. Every region had albinos without pigment or color who married there in their home region more times than not.

Although some of our Nigerian brothers and sisters are influenced by the extensive propaganda of the west these days, so too are we and yet Nigerians, African-Americans and all other Africans need to look inside our African culture more than following the west or anyone else blindly.

When you are in Warri, Sapele or any other costal Nigerian area or city, you may see some Nigerians with white blood in their veins but they are 100% Nigerian in culture and diet not western. You see light skinned brothers and sisters in Africa who do not feel superior just because of their shade of Black. Every region of Nigeria produces albinos who are without pigment and they range from light skinned to very light skin. Again, they are completely Nigerian in culture and diet. In Nigeria, people marry brothers and sisters from other tribal communities. And, if we think some one who is light is closer to white than we really do not understand that who we are as a people comes from within our

African soul. And, like our Nigerian brothers and sisters, we African-Americans produce all of the beautiful shades of Black.

We Africans all over the world have been producing all the beautiful shades of Black since the beginning of time and so shall it be in the future. Let us embrace the beauty of the diversity within us as a dramatic strength!

In the old brainwashed days some among us said if you are all right, if you are brown stay around and if you are black get back. But, let us teach ourselves and future generations that each and every shade of Africa is Black and Beautiful.

African people all over the world come from Africa. All shades of Black are African. All shades of Black are African historically and culturally and our color is our gift from Africa our motherland no matter what shade of Black it is. And, that is the importance of Africa, the source of Blackness that embraces all of us no matter what beautiful shades of Black we may be.

If we can practice a real love and respect for ourselves as a people then maybe our precious young people will value each other realistically instead of fighting and internal wars we see too often in our communities. Black is beautiful and it is so beautiful to be Black.

Why African-Americans Should Love Africa, Africans in America and Africans From All Over The African World and Other African-Americans with A Special Cultural Love

The Special Cultural Love

The special cultural love I speak of here should be specific enough that it is not confused with love shared in personal relationships, although since African-American men and women are finding it increasingly difficult to maintain viable relationships with so many brothers in jail, under court supervision in prison, unemployed, discriminated against, victimized by the USA White Supremacy State currently under the racist George Bush.

However, this special cultural or people's love in part covers the scope of personal relationship love, however, it is much wider than that yet it is crucial to our survival as an ethnic group because it is a special kind of love that people who have special cultural racial and kinship type ancestral ties born by the experience of being taken from Africa by force during the middle passage.

Although this is a call for a African-American wide special cultural love this is not a romantic love but should definitely include that kind of love too. However one must not ever give love without constantly monitoring and evaluating that love because that is the only way one can make sure it is mutual.

This is a special cultural love that recognizes that we were collectively victimized by foreign conquers and their armed forces - where we were forced to abandon on the rich cultural definitions and customs our people practiced for millions of years while free in our African homelands. We enjoyed that peace with our African people who were not kidnapped but who never the less were colonized, systematically divided for easy colonial subjection and fed a crock of lies about us their African-American brothers and sisters in the West from Chile to Canada and every where in between.

All of us individually are subjects of the International system of White Supremacy based in Washington, D.C., and London but stretching its tentacles around the world!

We Blacks whether in Africa, the Americas or even the Pacific Islands Black areas like Australia, Van Atu, New Guinea are getting the worst of the treatment from the International White Supremacy State. And, our status whether in individual partially liberated countries like Nigeria or New Guinea or Africans in America continues to be that of a colonized victimized people individually unable to win the fight against the International System of White Supremacy.

I am proposing that we Africans all over the world share a special cultural love with fellow Africans all over the world based on the common history and cultural, victimization of slavery and colonialism by the supporters of the ideology and practice of White Supremacy.

I am not proposing we love everyone who is Black only because they are Black because that could result in our folks continuing to be victimized by the self-haters among us. So we still have to be smart enough to determine if someone who portrays friendship to us Black or any other color is sincere and that is the qualifier and so vitally important!

And we have to be aware of the self-haters among us! So although we are speaking of a special cultural love among us, we note this is not a blanket love.

So if you love yourself you can love any other people or peoples who show you love and who are not actively oppressing you or your people.

Self-Haters

The pitiful fool is the one who loves everyone else and everything about everyone else but despises himself and people who look like him or even all of the women from his own family or African Population or African Community.

There are murderers among us who are self-haters. These self-haters are full of misguided hate for other Blacks specifically or generally because they hate being Black and African and sometimes love everyone and every thing else in the world. You can love anyone you want to but when you practice self- hate and self-destruction, you are a self-hater and self-haters are the worst people in the world because they keep shooting other African-Americans. Love anyone you like, but do not love a self-hater or be a self-hater.

The self-haters maybe conscious or unconsciously hate themselves and their condition as an oppressed people but chose to not address the issues that confront us or prepare themselves by learning how to read, write and compute so we can face our challenges.

The self haters instead aim their weapons and venom at our own people by choosing to pursue a life style that leaves our people as victims thrown all over the streets. The self-haters aim low in life while we need our young people to dream but also achieve in school as well as work so that more than street options will be available once adulthood presents itself. Africans born in America-young people or young African-Americans- Adulthood is definitely coming

Where your parents and our people will have rising expectations for you and as the late Malcolm X said the future belongs to those who prepare for it! We need to end the negative trend in the thinking of some of our people who say if you are acting smart in class or society that somehow you are acting white. This is a dangerous way of thinking, we as African-Americans can not allow us to achieve as much progress as we can in a time where we need progress so badly.

In order for our strong youth not to be traced or tracked into a self hater lifestyle, our parents need to constantly encourage our students to achieve at their highest possible potential for instance my parents always told us you have to be twice as smart to get half as far as the others not facing the challenges we face. "In our family that advice worked to produce my highly qualified brothers and sisters".

And, if you are a low achiever or self-hater, you hold the key to turning yourself around as an act of self-determination no matter what, no matter what your shade of black, social economic condition or learning obstacles.

You can be your own engine to expand your mind even if your family is not rich or well off if you apply yourself work, work hard and make sure you do your very best to complete all levels of preparation - All levels of school you possibly can.

Again, self love and a love of your family, self, community and people must come first with that as a proper foundation, you can love any other too based on merit!.

The reason it is so important for African-Americans in particular but African people in general to focus on self love is that the level of self inflicted violence murder and mayhem in our families communities and populations is totally self destructive and stems in large part from our slave/colonial past feelings of hopelessness, fear and in many cases feelings of extreme powerless to improve our destiny.

Elevating self-love to its highest level is not the total cure but it is part of the solution we need to redeem ourselves and our people from the disease of self hate. We do not have to be self-haters nor do we have to produce self-hating people. Better, we produce our people with self love not self hate so we can develop ourselves and love ourselves, love our people and love our origin and history of All African People. Then, we would be in the best position to love anyone else who loves us. Self-love is the cure for being a self-hater!

When we begin to openly and willingly love ourselves and our people, we will then be ready to work together better under a strategic National Black Consensus concept to chart a method, operational format and strategy to lift ourselves out of the negative aspects of our present mentality and progress towards a more united mentality and a more united state of mind as a people!

Many of our young people are challenged by self-destructive. Double negative of one hand expressing and feeling that acting like you are smart and intelligent in class while learning means somehow one is acting white. That kind of thinking holds back the beginning of intelligent and mature behavior. Sometimes this is a big factor in academic success.

Challenges. In general when faced with any learning situation like school we should always try our very best to be successful as intelligent African- Americans and also make sure we read our story out side of the classroom settings to better understand who we are and why it is so important for our young African-Americans to learn as much as we can from our people's 500 year history point of view and the view of the majority group in this country so we can better understand how to survive by working together in this situation we are and exist in called America!

We can carry that positive image ourselves based on a love of and knowledge of ourselves to our school, church and all through life!

Conclusion

African-American parents please buy this book for you, family and brothers and sisters in our community. You should also buy books by and about Black People locally, nationally and internationally for your house. Read and discuss this book with your family after all school and homework is done on a nightly/weekly basis in small pieces or a few pages at a time and have family discussions. Turn off the television for homework and the reading/family discussion hour.

Follow this method for reading African-American History books to supplement the majority group (white) public school curriculum so your families will not buy into this crazy but popular notion that if a Black person is smart they are acting white. Please help our people defeat such destructive notions so we can rise to meet and exceed our full potential!

Some Good Advice for African and African American Youth

Enjoy video or computer games but never more than 1 hour per day. Since the laws of the country mandate you, you must go to school. Make the best of it! Besides, this is the time and the only time you will have an all expenses paid opportunity to go to school. If you drop out your life choices will be very difficult. Life might be difficult if you try your best but life will be tougher on you if you do not try your best. Think of the other young people around the world who would love to go to school but may not have the opportunity before you tune out, drop out or get tired of doing your daily homework assignments! Graduate and make us all proud by mastering the white supremacy tainted education and read independently to learn about the mighty story of proud African People all over the world!

Don't buy into the negative assumption that if you show now intelligence you are acting white on the mostly white knowledge you must learn in school. Learn it! But, prepare yourself properly by reading about and discussing Black History with your parents, siblings and real friends. This way learning will not just be for schoolwork. Find your reading passion - what you like to read but every kid in the world especially of black kids need to learn about our positive inventions and contributions to the progress of mankind to balance the fact that you will probably now learn about Slavery and other aspects of the tragedy of Black Oppression from the white majority perspective.

Please stop using the N word by any spelling or emphasis because this is the insult poured on our ancestor for 100's of years even up to the 1960's by those who were injuring us, raping, robbing and killing us for breakfast, lunch and dinner!

Finally, stop sagging your pants, because no one but you should know the color and type of your underwear! Pull up your pants up to your waist and walk like our proud ancestors walked tall, proud and erect! You will not have to worry about your pants falling if they are secured on your waist with a proper belt. Then you really could walk as proud as our ancestors would have wanted us to when they might have been whipped by slavers for walking and standing proud

Lastly, code switch - speak home English at home street English in the street and classroom English in school!.

And, stop using the N word! Finally, please remember as a Black person with an African origin love! Africa is the place we all come from. Remember that hating Africa and yourself could make you a self-hater. Please do not be an N-Word using self-hater! Instead practice self-love; love for your people and any other person in the world who respects you! You must also love Africa, our place of origin to complete a positive self-image with a proper amount of self-esteem. And, learn African-American history while you are young!!!

The National Black Trust

My response to Dr. Uhuru Hotep's piece titled "Protest Politics and Jena Generation: Lessons for 21st Century Black Leaders! Hotep suggested Africans in America or African-Americans abandon Jena Style mass mobilizations while pooling some of our funds to buy what we need instead of only begging if I understand the piece correctly. I think I do, however, here's one important factor?

This new youth of today need to see and feel the power we as a people can generate, and the empowerment that can flow from us getting together as a people. This is truly a unique for a generation so used to only coming together foe a concert or funerals!

In the Jena Mobilization, we found a new generation of our people seeing the feeling of our people seeing the feeling of empowerment and feeling the power of African-American unity. In short the younger people of our stepped up and showed they have the guts to continue our historic March to Black Liberation., We can never take mass mobilizations off the table.

Mass mobilizations and protests as well as demonstrations are among our most effective tools politically, socially, culturally and even spiritually. If we begin planning these types of protest gatherings we can better plans how to make them more economically viable to a certain point. What we need to do is make sure we reap as many of the benefits as possible we are at the planning stage.

The reason we can never take mass demonstrations off the table is because demonstrating together is an act of political empowerment. And for our dis- empowered people who face a lot of frustrations, we need more empowerment than less!

We need all types of loving experiences with each other in a situation where due to feelings of powerlessness and frustration we nurture self hate with many of our people becoming active self-haters. Every type of positive get together that does a service to our people and keeps the forces of self-hate out of it helps to show us as a people, the power of our homogenous unity. Empowering demonstrations raises our collective profile in the minds of Africans all over the world but especially among ourselves. So we should never stop demonstrating until the last brother or sister is on their way to the bank, hopefully an African-American owned bank to cash their/our reparations check!

So I disagree with the thrust of the first pillar of Dr. Uhruu Hotep's ideas about abandoning the mass demonstration as a part of a comprehensive National Strategic Black Consensus on where we need to go as a people. However there is much I agree with much of where Hotep is coming from but we have to be comprehensive to be effective in our unique position.

However, I have a vision of how we can as Hotep says, in so many words to buy collectively in some way the things we need.

My 12 years of experience as a non-profit community organization administrator in San Francisco gives me a unique perspective on how this part of the plan - collectively buy what we need can be accomplished.

You see in our struggle, historic March to Black Liberation, we must continue a clarion call for reparations that will provide the most righteous form of empowerment however, while we press for reparations as a part of a strategic National Black Consensus, we should also establish a National Black Trust. This National Black trust could be formed on a National basis in the USA with governing board members in a Trust Constitution that limits terms of office to 2 - 2-year terms.

The National Black Trust could also be established in every state, region, county and city we live in as a significant population group.

Every brother or sister like Hotep could donate $400.00 per year to the local $50.00 to the State National Black Trust and $25.00 per year to the regional or county Black Trust , and $25.00 to the National Black Trust because the most important priority is local.

These trusts can give grants to self-empowerment community based efforts and enable small businesses of our people to survive!

So we can establish these trusts to give African-Americans with some money a way to contribute to buying instead of begging for everything we need as Hotep put forward.

However, we should never limit those of us with less money and more powerlessness an opportunity to participate the historic and National Liberation March by discontinuing empowering demonstrations.

We all need a way to participate in our National Liberation effort by loving each other locally, seeking empowerment through mass demonstrations, building national, county or regional, statewide, and local city wide trusts. We should build trusts and continue to push for reparations as a people to implement a strategic National Black Consensus to move our people from powerlessness to empowerment so that we can take power in our lives, communities and regions.

This strategic National Black Consensus will also prepare us to take an appropriate amount of National Power and raise our African-American profile around the world. Once we do make these moves we will be prepared to participate in a world wide African conversation or 8th and 9th. All African People's Congress and actually have something to brag about while embracing our people all over the world!

Footnote: I responded to in the last 6 or 7 pages to Protest and Jena Generation Lessons for 21st Century Black Leaders written by Dr. Uhuru Hotep of the Kwame Ture - Leadership Institute

Assignment:
Go to
http://www.youtube.com/watch?v=uPz7xAnLF9M and view the 7-minute video.

Click on the video button and watch all of the video clips from the bottom one up!!!

http://www.youtube.com/user/ukalitheafrican
http://www.nathanielturner.com/larryuklaijohnsonreddtable.htm

Spoken Word should be spoke and heard

Going Through

Give the world a surprise
Unite Blacks before Sunrise
Then despite
That we are despised
We would show
We are wise
Up end deadly disunity
in our community
Give a living brother
Some immunity
Despite what we
Are going through
We have to do
What we have to do
For the sake of
Our Black Destiny
See the need
For our people's unity
Give the world
A surprise
Unite Blacks
Before sunrise

A More United Mentality

Hit by Katrina
6 in Jena held
Ignored by neglectful FEMA
San Francisco 8 in Jail

Three strikes
The third rail
Too many of us
Held in a jail cell

Our disunited
Mentality
And another
Brother to brother fatality

Our blood runs
That is a reality
We face white supremacy
Without Black Unity

NYPD filled Sean Bell with 50 bullets
That is police brutality
That twisted warped insanity
In our reality

The SFPD in its stupidity
Shot Lumpkin and the late Idress
In the SF Metreon brutality
But where is our united mentality?

And we see this
Coast to coast
None can boast
Through it all keep standing tall

In this insanity
Where is our unity?
When we shoot
Each other like an enemy

In this time
No need to rhyme
Unite our mentality
To change our reality

Too ignore Black Unity
In this insanity
Unite my people
Unite our mentality

United State of Mind

United state
of mind
is what we
must find

For our kind
One love one mind
Black Love
Black rhyme

United
in head
Feed those
Underfed

Seek Unity
Black Community
Black on Black
Murder is insanity

A united
state of mind
means progress
for our kind

Working for us
To be together
Unity is better
My sister and brother

So we can make
The killing stop
Before another
Brother drop

Look for what
We must find
Unite our
State of mind

Unity
Black Community
So we don't bleed
Because of stupidity or greed

Unite our
State of mind
Among our kind
Unity we must find

SCHOOL IS COOL

Use school
Your best learning tool
Cause you must realize
School is cool

Learning is fun
And must be done
when you are young
Learn and run

You can learn
Good grades you can earn
School is your chance
So you can advance

In school
Obey the rule
Learn English and Math
School is cool

Go to the library
Read whole books
Shower before school
Groom your looks

The best thing
A student can do
Learn to read and write
With all your mite

Let no one say
Learning is not cool
Destroy your future
And make you their tool

Learn in elementary,
Middle and high school
Remember the rule
School is cool

Think of college
Or your next step
Don't answer that cell phone
Or send that text

Use school
Your best tool
Remember the rule
School is cool

Juneteeth 2009 We Are Black History

To the mighty
3/5ths unequal
The mighty
Juneteeth People
This is
Our special day
To say
In our special way
We are here and
Obama, Obama, Obama leads the way
With Michelle
In the white house today
Through trials
And great tribulation
We fought on for
Our Black liberation
To the mighty
3/5ths unequal
Listen and learn well
Hear me my people
Love or at least respect
Everyone
No matter where
they come from
Embrace Black Self Love
My beautiful people
So we can be alive and
have a sequel
for our ancestors from Africa
To our ancestors all over America

No Chains on our
Hands and feet
They even say
We are free
To the mighty
Juneteeth People
We will be equal
And Obama, Obama, Obama is our sequel
This is our story
Our days of Black Glory
You And Me—WE
Are Black History

People's Love

Where is our people's love
Blessed by God above
When we kill each other
my sister and brother

First love yourself
Then love God our maker
Then love self and kind
In the killing fields of our communities
Do not be a faker

First love ourself and kind
One love, we must find
Then we could love everyone else
But first we must show a love of self

Once we love our self
and stop killing each other
begin anew as a people
To show real love

To each brother
and love not mistreat our sister
It will be so easy
to love any other

Find our people's love
In our heart or in God above
One love, my people
then freedom is our sequel

Stop Sagging

Stop sagging
Brothers
Stop sagging
Brothers and others

If you know
Who you are
A young man
A young African

Wear your pants
Above or at your waist
Show class
And taste

Wear your pants
Above your butts
Be a real Black Man
Please understand

Sagging shows
Your private
Wear pants
To hide it

That area is meant
To be covered
The color of you underwear
Should not be discovered

Showing your butt
Is indecent exposure?
Wear your pants on your
Waist, show class and taste

MAKE IT STOP

All over the
African-American Nation
We must unite
To seek liberation
Cause Black on Black crime
Is a shame!
When freedom
Is the name
Of the game

Stop the crazy killing
Or continue the pain
We're feeling
Risking our destiny
Dieing over community
All over our nation
Black on Black killings
On the rise
All over our nation
Hear mothers and sisters cries

And brothers
We can make the killing stop
Practice peace in the hood
On every block
Stop killing your brother man
This is our people's demand
So we can assassinate
Discrimination
And take our liberation

And take our piece of the rock
In this white man's nation

So brothers on every block
Come together
And make the killing stop!!!

Stop Using the N word

Stop using
the "N" word
We are more
Profound than that
And we are proud
To be African and Black
Aren't you proud of that
Stop using The "N" word
In school or in the office
Using the N word
is not a good practice
We are much more
Profound than that
And proud to be
African-American and Black
Stop using the "N" word
Proud and mighty people
One day we will be equal
Stop using the "N" word
As we struggle for equality
In our streets,
Home and community
Stop using the "N" word
We are more profound
Than that Proud African,
African-American and Black
It is a shame
We don't have more game
Than to wear the N word
As our name

The N word
Should never be heard
Don't use the N word
Don't use the N Word
Don't use the N word
No matter what
You have heard
Don't use the N word
Have some pride
STOP AFROCIDE
Despite whatever you heard
Don't use the N Word

Bring Back One Love

Bring back
One love
Stop the flow
Of Black Blood

For the lives
Of the Black Man
And the souls
Of Black Women

For the children
For our friends
For our sisters
For our kin

Bring Black
One Love
Stop the flow
For Black Love

In the name
Of our father above
Re-discover
One Love

Moms keep
On crying
Sons keep
on dying

The pain
Is growing
So we should
Be knowing

Bring Back
One Love
Silence all
Of our guns

Bring Back
One Love
Don't stand
In a brother's blood

Bring back
One Love
Look at what
We have done

Bring Back
One Love
We are drowning
In our own blood

Bring back
One Love
End the flow
Of Black blood

When brothers
We could
Bring back
One Love

Let go of
The rudeness'
Bring back
The smoothness

Bring Back
One Love
Bring Back
The coolness

Stop the flow
Of Black Blood
Bring back
One Love

African Awareness

Black Awareness
For those who have
Lost consciousness
Too many are aimless

Too many are hopeless
Too many homeless
However stress in part
From being goal less

Feeding African Awareness
For those lacking
Higher consciousnesses
The aimless and the hopeless

Reasoning ends conflict
And Black on Black murder
Must surely cease
From the west to the east

Let the flow
Of our blood desist
Ignorance is deadly ugly
And surely not bliss

Don't beat a brother
With a hand or fist
Don't twist
A sister's wrist

Stop shooting bullets
Into a brother's soul
African Blood brothers
Don't be so cold

With a new
Black awareness
Don't be so cold
Rejoin the fold

Embrace Black awareness
Unite and express
A new African Awareness
Embrace aims not aimlessness

Instead of claiming
Or embracing the N word
Reclaim the Blackness
Celebrate our African Awareness

Let A Sister Be Praised

Let a sister
Be raised
Let a sister
be praised

Not just noting
Oppression
This a positive
Expression

From the ash heap
Of white history
To the queendom
Of African History

From the segregation
Of the white nation
To the top of
Our African Nation

Let a sister
Be raised
Let a sister
Be praised

She is our diamond
In the rough
She survived so beautiful
Our sister is rough

She is our
Treasure chest

She is unique
And she is the best

Through abuse
And scorn
From us our
Sister was torn

Cause she is
Special to us
I am
Serious

Let those who dare
To keep a sister down
Find a way
To rise from the ground

Lift our sister up
Lift her image too
Sisters you know
We need you

Don't put our sister down
In your city or town
Don't be a fool
Cause sisters are cool

Let a sister
Be raised
Let a sister
Be praised!

See It Soon

Making Martyrs
Is our doom!
May we see
May we see it soon

Not just for
A tune
Another one falls
As bullets fly zoom zoom

When we could
Wear our throne
Shooting through
A brother's dome?

A realization
Must surely come
Can we realize
What has been done

Black Death
Is an ugly tune
Black Destiny
May we see it soon

Open our eye
Regain our pride
Black Folks unite
And watch us rise

Can we see
A brighter day
Can we sort it
Out a better way

Self-genocide
Fratricide
Let Black Love
Help us survive

When eyes are dried
When we find our pride
When we unite
We will thrive

May we open!
Our eyes
So we
Can rise

Shooting each other
Is our doom!
OPEN OUR EYES
AND SEE IT SOON

Who Are We (1998 Version)

Who are we?
Who are We?
Are we bad students?
Are we bad students?
No, No, No, No
We are Very good students?
We are very good students?

Who are we
Who are we
Are we terrible students?
Are we terrible Students?
No, No, No, No
We are very good students!!
We are very good students!!

Who are we
Who are we?
Are we good students
Are we good students?
Yeah, Yeah, Yeah, Yeah
We are very good students!
We are very good Students!

The Beauty of being Black

Through the
back door of history
Required to sit at
the back of the bus

the challenges
for you and me
but we
control our destiny

Being one
of a kind
In control
of our mind

Subjected to
Them and their rules
We're free in our mind
We are no fools

They push us down
But we rise again
That's the beauty
Of being Black my friend

Though America is
Totally whack
There is beauty
In being Black

They press us down
Oppressed people

wear a frown yet
let liberation be found

Never forget
Never regret
Rejoice unite
And raise your voice

My brothers in prison
We win with reason
Whether it's hard
Or easy in this season

We know it's hard
Some can't find
A job

An economic
Recession
And
white oppression

They push us down
But we rise again
This is the beauty of
Being Black my friend

Though America
Is totally whack
There is beauty
In being Black

ALL THE KILLING

All the killing
must to cease
So there can
Be peace

End all military
And police occupation
Free our people
Give them liberation

Or just leave
Them alone
Let them work it out
On their own

The killing of
The Black man of the east
Must cease
so there can be peace

In the Sudan
Home of the Black Man
In Africa
Home of the Black Woman

Let peace
break out
In the west
And the east

Let the
killing stop
let the
violence drop

the Black on Black killing
must cease
so there can
be peace

All the killing
must cease
so there
can be peace

Congratulations to the newly independent state called South Sudan born out of a 21 year fight against Sudan the state in the northern part of that area. Sometime there must be separations so we can get in the right regions bur we should hope for a United States of Africa

Find The Way

When we
Find the way
Better will
Come that day

Find a way to
love each sister and brother
with the passion
of the love of a lover

So we have
To hold on
Until we get
united and strong

one brother
united with the other
treating ourselves
much, much better

Hear me
My sister
Hear me
my brother

An undying love
To share together
Then we'll be
United forever

When we all
Find a way
Better will
come that day

Can't sit
On the fence
Black Love
Is common sense

You know its way
To tense
And Black Love
is common sense

Our brothers
we lay down
Our sisters, mothers and families
Cry and frown

When we all
Find the way
Better will
Come that day

The toll and the cost
When another brother is lost
When we pull the trigger
Fool and gravedigger

When we all see
We are not our enemy
Black Love will shine that day
You know we cannot wait

Start today cause
we when we
find the way
Better will come that very day

Hear what I say
To God we pray
Find the way
And better will come that day

LOVING BLACK WOMEN

Your beauty
Is legendary
Sweeter than the
Sweetest berry

For as long
As we remember
You have our child
Please deliver

When you were made
God did a good thang
I was so happy
I sang

And thanked
our maker
and then we begged
Please never take her

Since that day
What can I say
We have been understand
Loving our Black Woman

Your sweet lips
Are heavenly
Baby you are so
Special to me

Loving our Black Woman
For standing by us
Love for our Black Women
From the Black Man

Loving our sister
For standing by us
Loving our Black Woman
Loving you is a must!

Love the Black Woman
For the love
She is giving
While she is living

Giving you flowers
while you are living
we appreciate
The love you're giving

Loving beautiful
Black Women
Sister understand
This is the love of a Black Man

Thank God For You Mom!

We thank God's giving
For every day you are living
And we love you so
Let the world know

This is a prayer
To keep you here
Healthy and God fearing
In this world living

For you we pray
To God every day
We love you mom
And thank God everyday

Not thinking of Pilgrims
or slavery in our past
Thanking God for you
Is our only task!

Because we are family
Mom gave us unity
We love you now and
We'll love you for eternity

This is God's day
We share what we say
We love you Mom
Each and every day!

We eat the food
We share today
And love you God
To you we pray

We are serious
Together this day
Mom we express our love
This thanks giving day

Feel Beautiful

On a cool
Tree lined street
Sounds and smells
And soon the beat

UC Davis
Black Family Day treat
With the beautiful sisters
You see and meet

May our ancestors
May 19, 2007
Be remembered
In heaven

Feel beautiful
Today
The sun shines
This way

And our spirits
Are united
May the wrongs
Be righted

To our sisters
who are dutiful
Please my sisters
You are beautiful

To our brothers
Get on the right thing train
Please develop
your intelligent brain

So many beautiful
Sisters
Walking around
Our sister's beauty
is profound

Malcolm X's
Birthday
A soldier
Who showed the way

Feel beautiful
Not the sad situation
Feel beautiful
Unite for Liberation

African-American History 2007

Taken on
a slave ship
Licked and hit
by the slave ship

This is my people
3/5th's unequal
We struggle
For a sequel

And now we have turned
On ourselves
Can we do
something else

Taken from our Kinship
Taken on a slave ship
Whipped and hit
How can we forget?

Marching into 2007
Will we make it to 2011

Too many brothers
Killing each other
My brothers
Can we do better?

Taking each other out
Weakens our people's clout
Emerging from the insanity
Of being treated like the America's enemy.

We got
To live
To love the love
We live

A gun is
A slave ship
A gun is
A master's trip

Be more united
So we can live
So we can love
The love we give!

Our people's will
Is that we heal
Our people's will
Keep it real

Among each other
And our black family
Can we unite
For black Destiny

Can we give
Love and unity
And work together
With creativity

And bring together
Our sister
And
Our brother

For a positive endeavor
Can we work together
In African-American History 2007
To survive until 2011

In need of unity
In need of Harmony
Remember we share
One Destiny

Young Brother/Young Man

By Larry Ukali Johnson-Redd

Listen to "Your World
And Mine" by Luciano
Check out Mutabaruka
And Brother Baraka

Forget Condi Rice
Checkout Paradise
Open the door, listen to
Old School by Terry Moore

Get some wisdom and pride
You ought to
Listen to Sundiata
Use your mind to save our kind

Get some love
In your heart
Let us have
A brand new start

Listen to Malcolm X
Listen to Marvin X
Project
giving a brother respect

Stand proud
My young brother
Please don't kill
Any other

Seek wisdom and truth
Uncover our Black root
Show you are aware
Stop Black on Black warfare

Check out
Linton Kwesi Johnson
Chuck D
And the Jr. Fred Hampton

Read Chancellor B Williams
And John Hedrick Clark
Marcus Garvey
And read some Ukali

Your road is harder
We can all see
But the sweeter
The victory

When we stop
Killing we
And work together
For our destiny

Get some education or training
To find a way to survive
Then we can all thrive

Get respect so
we can reject
The murder of a brother
By another brother

Listen to the voices
advising you
There is more than 1 way
To do what you must do

Our life is too valuable
To die like a fool in a fable
Live for our maker/ancestors
Live because we are able

Live a meaningful life
Marry a beautiful wife
Learn how to survive
So we can thrive

Listen to Sanchez
And progressive reggae
Let peace breakout
United we do have clout

Linking strong Black Arms
And strong Black Hands
So we can make it better
For all Africans

Young brother
Young man
Be a lover man
And friend

How nice it will be
Show love my young brother
No more bloody war
Among each other

Hear the drumbeat
Of our reality
Ignore insanity
Accept maturity

Think before you shout
Why should we beat our brains out?
This is wisdom, the freedom route
Divided we have no clout
United we will conquer without a doubt

Get some wisdom in your head
Make sure you are spiritually fed
No more standing in our own blood
Show your young brothers real love

Wise up stay tough
Ease up stay rough
Prepare your mind
Self-love we must find!!!

It's not easy
From a boy to a man
But can you make
If you don't understand

We cannot survive
without peace in our hood
When our blood runs
You know that's no good

Find some knowledge
To hold on to
If not,
We are through

As long as you
are a young man
Find self-love
Please understand

May you live long
Peace upon the land
Mature and grow up
Powerful young Black Man

Today's boy is
Tomorrow's Black Man
Please develop your mind
And grow old in this time!!!

I challenge all young brothers between 15 to 24 years to memorize this long spoken word piece as a part of making a smooth transition from boyhood to manhood. Please look up the books, media and authors mentioned and you will obtain an even deeper understanding of this piece. I hope you enjoyed this piece and I hope you and your family will read my books and view or listen to my media. All of my books and media can be viewed, reviewed and purchased on my website by clicking on the media ordering button on this website's web page. May all young men read, understand and grow old in this time.

When My Ancestors Speak To Me!
Dedicated to the San Francisco 8 and all African-American Political Prisoners
As well as Middle Passage and MAAFA Black Holocaust Survivors

Those tortured
Must be compensated
Those tortured by racism
Must be paid

Those oppressed
By the country and the state
Culture/Language taken
Our humanity forsaken

5/5ths of a human
Never 3/5ths
Slavery based
On white lies and fibs

PAY REPARATIONS
To Black Nations
African-Americans first
Then affected Caribbean and African Nations

When you oppress
A whole nation/population
You must pay
REPARATIONS

To the home
Of the brave
Built on the labor
Of the African slave

Take responsibility
For the slave raid
And Reparations
Must be paid

To build up
White wealth and nation
You enslaved
the African Nation

TAKE RESPONSIBILITY
American Nations
Pay Slave descendants
Pay Reparations

Remove this stain
And American shame
You paid the Cali Japanese
Compensate for the chain

And for those
Tortured
Like the San Francisco 8
Don't be fake compensate!

Compensate
Political Prisoners
REPARATIONS

TO ALL BLACK NATIONS

Condemn the chains
and the hangman's noose
White only bathrooms and bosses
And those burning crosses

Condemn slavery
And big white lies
And whites got rich
And stole our sisters thighs

Condemn 3/5ths lie
We call it Genocide
Condemn the confederate Flag
To us it a dirty rag

There must be
Condemnation
There must be
compensation

Pay Reparations
To all Black Nations
Pay Reparations
To Black Populations

Millions of Black Political Prisoners
Forced to live in chains
Ethnically cleansed of culture
Language and our names

America
only one-way
Can you pass?
The test today

And when you
If you pass this test
You will prove to be
Better than the rest

A people wronged
Must be righted
Is America Blind
Or will it be sighted

Be thoughtful
Not excited
Then the wrongs
Can be corrected

Pay Compensation
Black Reparation
To African Americans
And Harmed Black Nations

Taken from Our African Homeland
When our family got big land
In North Louisiana
The white man took that land understand

And my ancestors ran
North to Little Rock
And on to San Francisco where they were
Discriminated against some more

When My Ancestors Speak To Me

Another Night of Murder=Mother's Tears

Sitting in a quiet
Side of Oakland
Wondering why all the killing
My brother Black Man

Salutes to 118 plus
New ancestors mostly us
About partner murder
Can we close the door!

For the pain
The victim's family feels
For the loved one missed
Cause the bullet killed

As our blood flows
Is it really worth it
About this killing trend
Do you think we need it?

Blood flows
Like a mother's tears
Disputes unresolved
And young lives unlived

Can we make peace!
Oakland turfs west and east
Richmond and Frisco
Killing brothers no more

Resolve disagreements
Resolve arguments
We can work it out
cause united we have more clout

Can we love
each other
my sister and
Black brother

Murder is no
Resolution
For us Black on Black love
Is a better solution!

Can we work it out!
Or is it a must
Another dies
Another bites the dust

Am I the only one!
Feeling all of this
We can resolve it
Without a gun knife or fist!

What else
Can I say
Stop this killing
THIS VERY DAY

118 MURDERS
MOSTLY OF US
Killed by others
And our own brothers

Can a mother's love
End toward the child
She bears
who cares

When the killing
goes on and
Our home
Is a killing zone

Instead of shooting at each other
In Oakland's Black Nation
Focus on One Love and Reparations
Development and Liberation

We should be marching
Around Lake Merritt
Demanding Liberation
And a job and my reparation

Let The Love Show

My People our love
For each other
Must grow
My sister and brother

Grow our love
victims of the
Middle passage
We were ravaged

Brought to
The USA
Lynching us
From Africa

My people
Our love must grow
My People
Our love must show

Show sisters
And brothers
Let our love
grow and grow

Make sure you
Let our love show
Let everyone know
Let self-love grow

We survived
Times past
Let our love
Grow very fast

Let our love
Grow and grow
Let my brothers
And sisters know

Treat every sis
Treat every bro
Like they live
Right next door

Let the love show
Act like you know
Let the love flow
Let the love grow

Love each other
A whole lot more
Let the love show
Let the love flow

Let it flow
Let it Grow
Open the door
And let it go

Respect One Another

Respect One Another
Love One another
My sister and Brother
Let us get it together

No rescue
From Katrina
Official neglect
From Bush to FEMA

Love each other
My sister and brother
Scattered and divided
Better we be united

Whatever liberation
For our Black Nation
We will be free forever
When we are united together

Respect one another
My sister and brother
Love one another
Better we be together

No more Black blood
Should drop
The flow of our blood
We must make it stop

No more shooting bullets
Into a brother's soul
Don't make sisters cry
Keep those eyes dry

The times have come
Let us unite as one
To continue killing each
other is dumb dumb dumb

Unite our streets
In our community
Be smart not dumb
Unite so freedom will come

Respect one another
Love one another
My sister and brother
Let us get it together

United State of Mind

United state
of mind
is what we
must find

For our kind
One love one mind
Black Love
Black rhyme

United
in head
Feed those
Underfed

Seek Unity
Black Community
Black on Black
Murder is insanity

A united
state of mind
means progress
for our kind

working for us
to be together
unity is better
My sister and brother

So we can make
The killing stop
Before another
Brother drop

Look for what
We must find
Unite our
State of mind

Unity
Black Community
So we don't bleed
Because of stupidity or greed

Unite our
State of mind
Among our kind
Unity we must find

The Exceptional Black Woman

What is an
Exceptional Black Woman?
She could be short
or tall, large or small!

Like Congress lady Barbara Lee
Or even Congress lady McKinney
Or Maxine Waters of LA known
Locally, nationally or internationally

They run corporations, countries
And households
Yet still they appreciate
A beautiful red rose

They discuss ideas
Not people
Young girls prepare
To be their equal

They are Black Women
With a major endeavor
They are Black Women
Who are very clever!

From very little
Great efforts have gone far
They shine like
A beautiful Black star

Exceptional Harriet Tubman
And Exceptional Queen Nzinga
Of Angola
Do you know her?

Without the
Exceptional Black Woman
Barren would be the fate
Of man and the land!

Can The Millions On The Right Be Wrong?

Was the white right
Right during slavery
And working us like cattle
Holding us like property

Stealing free Africans
From free African land
Kidnapping us from Africa
Illegally taking us to America

Was the white right, right
Or can't they be wrong
Making profits on
My ancestor's bones

The white right is wrong
Continuing bloodshed in Fullujah
Facing American military might
Cheered on by the white right

Can the white conservative
Oppressive hostile right
Be wrong?????

Need For Unity

My brother My sister
Get your read on
Get your
Knowledge on

Read about
African History
the African-American Story
our people's pain and glory

Read about Malcolm X
And Kwame Toure
Queen Nzinga
In African Angola

Read about Harriet Tubman
Who freed many
Black Women/Black Man
Garvey and Haiti's Toussaint

About our march
From white slavery
To our freedom
And Black Destiny

Read about
our pyramids
Unite Black Adults
Unite Black kids

Embrace Black roots
Tell the truth
The unity of the Blacks
Is our fruit

Divided we are weak
United we are strong
Divided we are oppressed
United we are too strong

Back in our history
They feared our unity
The same way today
Division is stupidity

Get your read on
Get your knowledge on
Learn our history
And our need for unity

December 4th in Oakland

I am in Oakland
10th and Broadway
The Place is hopping
And full of flavor today

At the Kwanzaa Show
04 you know
with Toni Tony Tone
the show is on

Eye candy
All over this place
Music is blasting
There is a video casting

No hate ration
We are all together
Hundreds of
A sister and brother

They are playing
Are you thinking of me
Every one but me
Is on their feet

The music got the beat
The sisters
Are looking dreamy and sweet

Cause we can
Enjoy good times
While there is singing
rhythms and rhymes

Hugging old friends
Folks making ends
No rain in southern
California

Happy I'm born here
The San Francisco Bay
Cause it's cool in
Oakland today!!!!

There is a real
Good vibe
And unity in
Our Black Tribe

Written at the Dec. 4th Kwanzaa and Christmas Gift Show in Oakland
And dedicated to the beautiful attendees who enjoyed the show

Part 2 At the Black Fashion Show12-04-04

When sisters model
The music is bumping
The sisters walk
Jumping and humping

One of a kind styles
Everything moving
No time to talk

When sister model
Really something to see
Sisters look so good
Straight from the hood

Eye candy
Like a sister should
We are all watching
Like sweet cherry wood

When sisters model
The brothers will watch
Prance, walk and dance
We all take a glance

It's in their attitude
Did I say they look good
Straight from the hood
Like sweet cherry wood

It's in their walk
And their attitude
The walk and the mood

Moving On

Moving on
Right on
To a liberated future
From a slave past
Free at last?

Moving on
Past tribal war
Killing each other no more
Close that door

Moving on
Past sufferation
Moving on
To Black Liberation

Moving on
Right on
To our destiny
To a future free

After we find
African-American unity
We can start in
Our own community

Poem to Sister India Arie

One of the pretty
Black Women
Is India Arie
She is a real cutie
Chocolate queen
Know what I mean
Singing her songs
Is her thing!
See her on
Influences BET
Singing from the bosom
Of our very soul
Aware of her beauty
A real cutie and her voice
Makes her a voice of choice
Playing your guitar
How beautiful you are
India Arie, you cutie
African in America
A Black Super Star
Dipping from our
Cultural well
With our story
You tell so well
You're a blossoming
Black Rose
Singing your
Heart felt Prose

And your love of self
Flows from your soul
We feel it
Let you music unfold
My sister
India Arie
You are
A real cutie

I saw India Arie on BETJ on July 1, 2007

Close The Gap

Don't sit
In the back
And yap,
Yap, yap

Improve
Your grades
Bridge the
Achievement Gap

Don't act like you don't
Know how to act
When you can
Close that gap

Learn best right now
In your time
Learn now
Graduate and shine

Don't sit in the back
And Yap Yap Yap
Bridge the
Achievement Gap

Educate your mind
Learn knowledge of every kind
Take off your shades
And improve your grades

Don't sit in the back
And Yap Yap yap
Move to the front
And close that gap

Please don't
Be a fake
Try your best
To graduate

Don't bust a cap
Or fight Black on Black
Listen to this rap
And bridge that gap

Don't fall
In a loser's trap
When you can
Bridge that Gap!!

And if you
Drop out of school
You will
Live like a fool

Listen to this rap
This rap is the map
Make the most of school
Achievement too—is cool

Don't fight
In school
Learn together
That's real cool

Don't sit in the back
And Yap Yap Yap
Move to the front
And close that gap!!!

End Mental Slavery

Heal my people
Pursue Black Destiny
We are not our enemy
End mental slavery

Develop your mind
Unity we must find
Stop killing our kind
Unity must be in our mind

Heal with Self-love
Beware of self-haters
Check out and separate
The real from the fakers

End mental slavery
Feed your mind
End mental slavery
Self love and love for our kind

Unite against poverty and
The oppression of our mind
Real Black Unity
Our brother is not our enemy

End mental slavery
With in our mind
Stop the Black on Black
Murder of our kind

Study our history
Use righteous common sense
Work for Black Unity
Our brother is not our enemy

End the madness
Don't cause more sadness
Unite and be strong
Then we can right the wrong

Black Unity is
Black Destiny
Black self-love
for self and kind

Black Unity Festival

Make our life
A Black Unity Festival
For Black Survival
For a Black Revival

End the
Blood shed carnival
Better we have
A Black Unity Festival

Find the
Empowerment
We seek and need
Don't make a brother bleed

Seek a better
Understanding
Instead of fighting (each other)
We can be rhyming

Giving each other
Loving a sister and brother
We will be so wise
So our people can rise

Off deal ground
Self-love is profound
Black Survival yea
Black Unity Festival

Not a deadly game
Of seeking murderous fame
Causing our families pain
Causing our people shame

Not our blood
Washing down the drain
Or drying
To a stain

First we unite
Put liberation in our sight
Pursue liberation
For the Black Family and Black Nation

End the fratricide
And the bloodshed carnival
Better we have
A Black Unity Festival

Call and Respond

When we call
Please respond
We'll get stronger
And live longer

When I call
Please respond
Unite as one
½ the battle is won

Among each other
Sisters and brothers
Keep it locked on peace
North, South, West or East

When I call
Please respond
May we live longer
Love and be stronger

May we open
Our eyes
So we
Can rise

Rise above
Murder and mayhem
Embrace Black Unity
Prepare for Black Destiny

When I call
Please respond
We need unity
To defeat our enemy

Until the unity
Is found
We will go
Round and round

No way forward
With out unity
We will
go Round and round

No way forward
With out unity
Love each other
Unity for Black Destiny

Regime Change is Slavery

Colonialism
Is the same
As slavery
To us victim's misery

Slavery is
A foreign catastrophe
Put on us
By a foreign enemy

Colonial
And slavery
Regime Change
Colonial brutality

Colonialism is bloodshed
Slavery is oppression
Right wing Intervention
Is Regime change America's shame

Bloodshed in Iraq
To regime change
To dominate the oil
Poor soldiers toil

Like blood shed
During and after slavery
Developed and trade with nations
Don't bring them a tragedy

You are dead
Or do what white folks said
Where are our reparations
Our ancestors were never paid

Regime change
Is bloodshed!
Rightwing intervention
Is slavery with or without intention

If bloodshed
is what comes out?
That is the wrong policy
Regime change is slavery

Embrace and respect
Self-determination
Give the people of the world
True Liberation

End white American
Empire Dreams
And give reparations
To Black Kings and Queens

Get it Together
(In San Francisco)

It was
1992
They were
killing quite a few

The Rev Donald Green
Invited Ben Vereen
Many meetings with young brothers
Brought us all back together

Ben Vereen and Rev. Green
led the Peace March
From Fillmore, H.P./ Bay view
Potrero Hill Sunnydale and Lakeview

We all marched
together
Calling for a truce to
Murder of each other

They played
a rap son
We all in
the same gang

to promote a unity thang
to promote Black Self Love
and an end
to the pain

Our truce brought
Our brothers together
And cleared up
All of the stormy weather

Cause young brothers
Were killing each other
When we needed
To get it together

The Black Ministers groups and Black Community Activists worked together to bring young brothers in San Francisco together and end community against community warfare in1992. I remember brothers and sisters and I, demonstrating with 24 paper caskets on the steps of SF City Hall and a funeral on Oakdale where a thin blue line of police separated two suit bedecked groups of young brothers because the funeral of one group was in the heart of another turf.

My Spoken Word

My spoken word
Should be spoke and heard
I got that from Terry Moore
But I pushed it through the door

You are bigger
Than the N word
Spoken word
Must be heard

No more put downs
So we all be around
Let us be known
For the love we own

No matter your turf
Or your scene
Make Black Love
The biggest thing

Spoken word
Should be spoke and heard
I got that from Terry Moore
But I gave it 1, 2, 3 and 4

Cause we are
Bigger
Than the
N Word

Spoken Word
Should be
spoke
and heard

We are bigger
Than the N Word
Spoken word
Should be Spoke and Heard

Spoken Word
Spoke and Heard #2

The can't control
Spoken Word Behold
Let the truth be told
To our people young and old

Spoken Word
Must be Spoke and Heard
Uncontrolled
Our story is told

Spoken Word
In our authentic voice
They control some musicians
But not our voice and choice

Let Spoken Word
Bespoke and heard
Free as a bird
Our Spoken Word

Speak to our feelings
And warnings
Against self destruction
Promote self-love and self-protection

Recording artist
Must be heard
Don't let companies
Control Spoken Word

Spoken Word
Must be
Spoken
And Heard

Spoken Word
Must be
Spoken
And Heard

Another Self Love Poem

We'll learn the
Importance of Self-Love
Through casualties from internal conflict
And the flow of Black Blood

We 'll realize
The harmony of unity
As we prepare for
For victory

We'll arrive
At the gates of Liberty
But first we must
Find Black Unity

We all must
realize
one reality
in our lives

A beautiful people
In an ugly situation
Black on Black murder
Is no good for the Black Nation

We will rise
When we realize
We'll arrive at
the gates of liberty

But only
If we find
Black unity in our heart
And Black unity in our mind

Make Black Unity
A brand new reality
Not another self-love Poem
I know I'm flow in

I hope you are
Feeling and growing
Better we as a people
Be knowing

The importance of
Self love
To end the flow
Of Black blood

The Pulse of Liberation

Listen to
The African Pulse
Listen to drumbeats
African hearts have pulse

Our African heat pumps
Beats drum beats
Of Liberation
For people's African Nation

Many populations
Many African Nations
All Africans feel
The Pulse of Liberation

Drumbeats of Freedom
Beats in our hearts
For Black Liberation
To every African Nation

This is the concept
One African World
Including every African Man
Woman, Boy and Girl

Heart beats for liberation
Unite in every African Nation
The Pulse of Liberation
Drumbeats of our African Nation

To New Guinea and Fuji
In the East
Africa - American and
Brazil in the West

In many ways
We struggle for liberation
Rise up with unity and pride
Worldwide African Nation

In our music
Can you feel it
In our minds souls
And in lives, we need it

Unite in a vision
Of Black Liberation
Let our vision rise
Decide on Black Love Worldwide!

The New Black Power

The Power to be
Who you are
United in our community
Pursuing dreams eternally

Defining ourselves
Knowing our story
Loving ourselves
In failures and glory

Observing
The best of us
Our Ancestors
Are in the dust

Never slaying
Our own essence
Is basic
Common sense

Where we
Move forward
Reverse the game
Backward to forward

We must make
Our new reality
Through unity
With you and me!

May we
Shine our sun
May better
Come

May we
See our way
To a
Better Day

We'll make
Progress
Trying our
Best

Working it out together
The united way
Will bring about
The Better Day

We Can

Can Black
Relationships
Work
If we both try

Black Love
Will live
May Black Love
Never die

Can Black
Man/Woman
Relationships Work
The have worked
In the past
In the Future
We can make it last
Cause we can
Make it work

We are in
Control
We make it roll

We can make
Our love hot
Work together
So it's never cold

We can make
It new
So it won't
get old

We can make
It so good
And you know
We should

We can
Make it work
We can
Black Woman, Black Man

Snake and Vulture

In the Land
Of the snake and vulture
Respect Black Life
And Black Culture

Respect brother man
His mom and wife
Give respect and love
Don't take black Life

In the land
With Black Blood
On it's left
And right hand

Built on slavery
Of the African
Do you
Understand

The oppression
Of the Black Woman
And the Black man
From African Land

Our Blood
Flows in this land
Cause we are not
Hand in hand

In this land of the
Snake and vulture
Respect Black Life
And Black Culture

No Need to Rumble

No need to Rumble
There should be
No fights unless
It's for our rights

No need to Stumble
Hit or hitting a brother
In a rumble
While we as a people crumble

Our only fights
Should be for our rights
No fighting brothers
Avoid fighting others

Travel with respect
Our dignity we protect
Internal fighting among us No!
Freedom we must project

No need to rumble
No need to fight or stumble
No more fights
Unless for our rights

The Music

When we play
The music
No sheet music
We just do it

Real expressions
On our face
Deep in our soul
We're stepping out bold

Like our music
We are progressing
But about Black
On Black Homicide

We must decide
To stop it nation wide
As we die
We assist our genocide

We don't need
No sheet music
But our brain
We got to use it

Stop shooting
And killing
Each Other

If we can
work it out
We will
Have more clout

And make a way
For each other
One love my
Sister and Brother

We know music
Our brain, Use It
No script
My people use it

We love the
Music
Our brains
Nourish it

We'll love
The soul melody
If we live and love
In harmony

We'll dance
The power dance
Until we
Can all advance

Guns

They're giving guns
In our ghetto
Are we using them
To kill our brother

Too many guns
In our ghetto
Without knowledge
We point them at each other

Too many bullets
Killing our brothers
And our Sisters
Guns made by others

And we shoot
Straight into ourselves
Making our life
Into a living Hell

We need more Knowledge
Than guns
Brothers' need
Legitimate funds

Too many times
Our blood runs
As we kill each other
With these guns

Reach out
To a brother
We don't have to
Kill each other

Unity we will
Discover
When we
Unite together

They are giving out guns
In the ghetto
Guns made by others
Killing our Sisters and Brothers

Get Ready 2008

Get ready - Go
Prepare for freedom
Even in this
Kingdom

Go, Go
for Education
My Black Nation
For Black Liberation

Seek the path
Around the wrath
Of white supremacy
Faced by you and me

Get up and go
For preparation
Education
And then liberation

Never divided
Or undecided
Find the path
And get excited

You know we can
If united we stand
On our ancestor's shoulders
Black Woman/Black Man

Forward together
My sisters and brothers
It is our liberation
Uncover and discover

Never divided
Never undecided
We got to do it
United

Never divided
Never undecided
We got to do it
United

Never divided
Never undecided
We got to do it
United

Attitude

Attitude
Is every thing
African King
African Queen

Attitude
Is every thing
African Queen
African King

A good one
Is always best
So study and prepare
To pass the test

Study hard
And get along
Try to do what is right
Avoid what is wrong

Be smart
Don't be rude
Display a great
Attitude

Prepare for the day
You will graduate
Be real working hard
Don't be a false

Work and earn
You're self-respect
When you graduate
No regrets

Common Sense
And a good attitude
Respect yourself
Don't be rude

Be good and strong
With a positive song
Prepare for the day
You will be grown

Reparations and Liberation

You owe as
For banning the Drum
With heart beat
Africa we come from

You owe reparations
To Black Nations
But first of all us who survived
The middle passage

You owe us
Cause one dreary day
You stole us away
Only to mistreat us along the way

To New Orleans Police
Thought trained to kill
You didn't have
To kill my brother

You owe us for treating us
Like a threat
Work us hard
Until we sweat

And those stolen wages
as well the white rages
The day-to-day oppression
To steel our human expressions

And 400 years of oppression
Living with no protection
And 100 more years
Of trickery and deception

For innocent brothers
On death row
We must stand up
And say no more

You owe reparations
To our generations
To even the playing field
Liberation for the black Nation

If We Could?

If we could
Love each other
Like sister
And brother

We wouldn't be
Looked at as a fool by others
We would be
United sisters and brothers

We would be
Working together
In unity my sister
And brother

If only we
Could love each other
My people
Like sister and brother

We could build
Another pyramid
You know that
Is what we did

We could work
For our freedom together
Progress my sister
Rise up my brother

If We Would

If we could
If we would
Love each other
Like sister and brother

We would be
Better off my friend
Treat a brother
And sisters like Kin

If we would
Really love each other
Like sister and brother
We would really do it together

If we would
Love each other
We would
be closer together

In hard times
Like these
Can we be
More together please

We don't have
To fight each other
When we can love
Each other as sister and brother

If we would
Love each other
Instead of punching or
Shooting someone's brother

Unity on the block
And in our family
No more treating each other
Like an enemy

Instead of shooting
A brother down
His family cry and frown
We can have peace in town

Reach out to the other
Your sister and brother
Cause if we would love
Each other forever

We would
Really have it together

We Won't Be Denied
Written February 6, 2007

We won't stop
We won't drop
We are wrongly tried
But we won't be denied

We want real Freedom
In white man's kingdom
We are hog-tied
We won't be denied

The KKK
Is on a night ride
But we won't
Be denied

It is a
Matter of pride
We must live
We must survive

Lay off my sister
But we got our vibe
Still we won't
Be denied

We are strong
We will fight
On and on
Shine on Black tone

We have cried
America has lied
No we won't
Be denied

We got
our hand tied
We won't
Be denied

Our Ancestor's
Cried
Still we won't
Be denied

Facing
Genocide
We won't be
denied

Our ancestors
Had to run and hide
We won't
Be denied

We should treat
Each other
Like sister
And brother

It's a
Matter of pride
So we won't
Be denied

Oppressed
And terrified
Yet we won't
Be denied

Stand up
United with pride
So we won't
Be Denied

Back In The Day

Back in The day
You know the old school
When common sense
And Black awareness ruled

We did the
Harambee Shout
And black on black
We worked it out

We had Malcolm X
And Martin L. King
We were united
Without Bling Bling

We had our Afros
We had naturals
And it was understood
We had brother and sisterhood

Black on Black violence
Was called no good
We had love flowing
In our neighborhoods

Well, the time
Has come
Again to unite
As one

Cause brothers
In the hood
Are killing each other
And that's no good

The spirit of liberation
Unite our new generation
Spread unity about
We will win with out a doubt

Stop the murder
And war fare of Black on Black
Cause time has come
Again, unite as one

Tell the brother's
In the hood
Black on Black killing
Is no good

Black Proud and Intelligent

Don't call a sister
A B or h—you see
When you are both
Queen of our family tree

Bring your mind
Out of the fog
Don't call a sister
A female dog

Don't use the
B or h word
In spite of what
you might have heard

Don't call each other
B or H and
Fight in school
Or on the street

Choose to be
Intelligent and sweet
Don't call your sister
An h or a b

All my sister's
And brother's too
You'd better listen
To what I say to you

Come on my people
Please do the right thing
Call each other sister
Majestic African Queen

Our family and ancestors
We must represent
Choose to be
Black Proud and Intelligent

Peace Among Us

Don't be
A wolf pack
Attacking
Your brother Black

Don't be
A wolf Pack
Acting
Like that

Be a wolf Pack
For justice
Propose unity
For just us

I'm talking to you
Whatever you do
Prepare you must
And peace among us

Learn as much
As you can
Black boy
Become a Black Man

We have No clout
If young brothers
Take each
other out

Help young brothers
To see
Ignorance is
Our enemy

Let a
Young brother read
Instead of
Making him bleed

Young brothers
Need to breed
Young brothers
Carry our seed

Preparation
Comes first
Liberation
Comes second

You won't live
Till the time is right
Dying from
a stupid fight

Let a brother
Read
Don't make
A brother bleed

Don't be
A wolf pack
Attacking
Your brother Black

Prepare
You must
For Peace
Among us

Calling

Calling on
African Kings
Calling on
African Queens

For a people's
Congress
So we
Will progress

Calling on Africans
Calling Caribbean's
Brazil/Guiana
And African-Americans

Not calling
Exploiters
Not calling
Oppressors

Calling on Mr. Aristide
The late Fela Kuti/Mandela
Calling Oba Eradiwa

Calling Africa for a
People's congress
For our peace
For our progress

Calling on
New Guineans
And all
Melanesians

Show your love
For Lumumba
Show your love
For Nkrumah

Nzinga of Angola
Nyerere
And Haiti's
Aristide

For the love
Of Malcolm X
For the love
Of ourselves

Calling Freedom
Loving Africans
For more unity in
Our community

Calling for unity
Calling for progress
Calling for an 8th and 9th
African People's Congress

Show your love
For Marcus Garvey
Farrakhan and
The late Stokley Sekou Ture

Calling on my people
For the real
An 8th and 9th People's Congress
You know the real deal

African-American History 2007

Taken on
A slave ship
Licked and hit
By the slave whip

This is my people
3/5th's unequal
We struggle today
For a sequel

And now we have turned
On ourselves
Can we do
something else

Taken from our Kinship
Taken on a slave ship
Whipped and hit
How can we forget?

Marching into 2007
Will we make it to 2011

Too many brothers
Killing each other
My brothers
Can we do better?

Taking each other out
Weakens our people's clout
Emerging from the insanity
Of being treated like the America's enemy.

We got
To live
To love the love
We give

A gun is
A slave ship
A gun is
A master's trip

Be more united
So we can live
So we can love
The love we give!

Our people's will
Is that we heal
Our people's will
Keep it real

Among each other
And our black family
Can we unite
For black Destiny

Can we give
Love and unity
And work together
With creativity

And bring together
Our sister
And
Our brother

For a positive endeavor
Can we work together
In African-American History 2007
To survive until 2011

In need of unity
In need of Harmony
Remember we share
One Destiny

Tennis Shoes

What a way
To make the news
Another young brother
Dies in Tennis shoes

On the streets
Let's drop it
You know
We got to stop it

Unite with a truce
Far and wide
We are dying
From homicide

We have to
Reverse this tide
We are making
Our own genocide

If it's fire
It is higher
On the news
Food chain

But here it is
A terrible thing
Black blood is
Worth more than Bling Bling

If it bleeds
It leads
Our blood is
Down the drain

Young brothers
Dying in tennis shoes
Is the only way
We make the news

But it's giving
Our Mother's
And Sister's the blues
When our young are dying and in the news

When a young
Son is buried
In stylish
Tennis shoes

Let's express
Our views
Find a new way
To make the news

Black Destiny

What are we
Going to be
Can we unite
For Black Destiny

What do we
Want to be
We want to be free
For Black Destiny

We need
Much more unity
To achieve
Black Destiny

Where ever
We are
You know
We are a Black Star

We don't want
To oppress any one
We want our freedom
To come

Stop the blood flow
Learn where to go
In our spiritual wisdom
We find the route to freedom

When we find unity
From Africa
To the Caribbean Sea
Black Destiny

From Brazil
To Chicago
To Lagos
All our folks

From Melanesia
May we be free
First unity
Then Black Destiny

In The Heart Of Our Youth!

Random violence
Black on Black Homicide
We are dying from
Self inflicted genocide

Self-Inflicted Genocide!!!

Partner murder
Black on Black Crime
We must end it
So our sun will shine

102 killed in Oakland
Yet it is only October 06
2 sisters shot
1 killed and 2 critical

Call it a cycle
Call it murder on sight
Call if off brothers and sisters
In no way it is right

And who is killing
Our people
In the heart of Oakland
In the heart of Richmond

We need a new
Black love
In the heart
Of Oakland/Richmond

We need a new
Black Love
In the heart
Of our youths

We are bleeding
We are dying
We know
That's the truth

Take the guns
From the killers
Of our people
Or have no sequel

Take the bullets
From the Killers
Of our people
Or have no sequel

Celebrate our Heritage
Written in January 2007

Celebrate
Our heritage
In this
Modern age

Celebrate where
We come from
Build Black Love
One by one by One

More Black Unity
Our brother
Is not
Our enemy

Celebrate
Our heritage
In this
Modern age

Proudly
Survived our past
Unite and break
The die that is cast

Cease Black
On Black killing
So we can progress
Begin the healing

Celebrate the march
Our ancestor's made
When they tried
To make a Black a slave

Celebrate our
Critical Thinkers
Black History
To African Destiny

Celebrate our
Beautiful skin
Unite and
We shall win

See us
Together
Brothers and Sisters
United forever

Reach and
Find
The power of
Our mind

Celebrate
Our heritage
Our heritage
In this modern age

Celebrate our history
Celebrate our heritage
Even though
We are in a modern age

Positively
Improve our future
Despite the Oppressor
The culture vulture

Celebrate our beautiful
Black woman
Celebrate our
Black Man

Work together
For our survival
Have a Black
Love Revival

Celebrate
You and me
Celebrate
Unite be free
Celebrate
Our heritage
In this modern age

Knowledge and Wisdom

May knowledge come
To the rejected one
May wisdom grow
We are no longer Negro

We know where
We began
We'd better know
Where we are going

May we have knowledge
May we have wisdom
Living inside
The white man's kingdom

Can we find
A way
To reason
This very day

Share the knowledge
Our roots and wisdom
Solve our problems
Reason in this season

We can stand together
For now and forever
We can unite
My sister and brother

Let us enjoy peace
In the west and east
So united together,
we can Struggle for

May we seek
Knowledge and wisdom
May we unite as a people
In the 'white man's' Kingdom

Attitude #2

I saw a sister
With her head down
Thought about Tupac
And self-love to be found

Feed her some food
Speak nice not rude
Show a sister gratitude
Change a sister's attitude

Take a sister
To a higher platitude
Just by being nice
Instead of being rude

Give a sister redemption
And you redeem yourself
Brothers love your self
Before you love someone else

Help a sister
Pick up her head
You hear the song
Keep your head up: Tupac said

Find something
Good to say
To our sister
This very day

Then when you see
Her on her way
She can smile and
Have something nice to say

Feed her some food
Speak nice not rude
Show a sister gratitude
Change a sister's attitude

When Did You Repent

When did you
Repent
For the slavery of yesterday
And oppression of today

When did you pay?
Reparations to my ancestors
Only to buy and sell
And now my brothers are in jail

When did you
Apologize?
Since 400 hundred years or more
Ago of lynching and tears

When did you pay
Reparations?
For the middle passage
Isn't that savage?

And when did you
Seek to restore
The people on who
You closed the door

When, When, When
Where, Where, Where
Will America pay?
Reparations today!

In our situation
Remedy stealing Black Liberation
America must repent
And pay Blacks Reparations

Love Your Mother

Love your mother
Love your father
My sister
And brother

You may not
Always see it
eye to eye
Don't ask why

You may or may not
do things together
Like sister and brother

Help keep
Your family together
Love your father
Love your mother

Launch your start
But don't break
Dad and Mom's
Heart

My sister
and brother
Love your father
Love your mother

Black father
Black mother
Love your child
Our little sister
Or brother

Love in our family
And love in our community
Sister and brother
Love your father and mother

Shades of Black

North South West or East
Shades of Black Live in peace
Beautiful Black faces
From many different places

All shades of Black
North south East or West
All shades of Black
Our beautiful shades of Black

In Canada
All shades of Black
All over the USA
All shades of Black

North South West or East
Let us live in peace
North South East and West
We must try our very best

In Africa
all shades of Black
In Papua, New Guinea
All shades of Black

In Brazil
All shades of Black
In the Caribbean
All shades of Black

The beauty rages
In all growth stages
Our African basis
The beauty in our faces

Beautiful shades of Black
All shades are beautiful
Black is Black
That is a fact

Beautiful smiles
On millions of Black faces
Beautiful shades of Black
In many different places

In Europe
Many shades of Black
All over the world
That is a fact

Our Story

Telling
Our Story
Our pain
Is our glory

And how we
Survived
In their oppression
And learn to thrive

In the face
of slavery
and even
Genocide

First the ride
In the slave ship
Only to be greeted
By the white man's whip

Picking cotton
And wealth building
We were beaten
to death-killing

Turning free people
Into slaves
Slaves lay in
Unmarked graves

Our predecessors
Our ancestors
Our link to our throne
Africa is our home

And our history
Surviving slavery
Treated savagely
Number 1 Public Enemy

Pursue our
Destiny
But first
Black Unity

Give us
The power to see
The strength that
Comes from Black Unity

Learn our story
Prepare for our Black destiny
The road for you and me
Leads to Black Unity

End mental slavery
With a united state of mind
A more united Mentality
Preparations for Black Destiny

No way forward
With out unity
We will go
Round and round

No way forward
With out unity
Love each other
Unity for Black Destiny

What If

What if
Brothers and sisters
United
And worked for wrongs to be righted

What if
Sisters get along
With each other
And loved a sister and a brother

What if brothers
Got along with brothers
Then brothers and sisters
Could have more love for each other

What if among us
The young respected the old and
The old respected the young
And among the young, they got it together as one

What if
We got it together
As it a united Sister and brother
What if; what if; what if???

End the White American Empire Dream

700 US Military bases
Around the world USA White man
12 billion dollars a month for aggression
In Irag and Afghanistan

End the American empire dream
Stop trying to be
The world policeman
Enforcing White Supremacy understand

End the empire
Pay Blacks reparations
End the empire white man
The world years for liberation understand

End the empire dream
Bring US troops home
Pay Blacks reparations
Do not mimic Ancient Rome

Give the world
A new relationship
End International White Supremacy
Flip the current script

Then watch the African World
Emerge from White Supremacy
End IMF War and American aggression
Let the world be what it wants to be

And to descendents of slaves
Whose ancestors are buried in unmarked graves
PAY REPARATIONS
To the African-American Nations

You can fall from your throne
And bust your dome
You can copy the fools
Of ancient Rome

Unite Black People

Unite Black People
From the suite to the street
Unite Black People
Stand up on our feet

Unite Black People
In our community
Where ever we live
My People in unity

Unite Black People
Love on the Black Street
Love Black People
Even in the suite

Unite Black People
Unite in our mind
Unite Black People
Unite Self and kind

Unite Black People
Focus on Black Progress
Unite Black People
For our success

Unite Black People
Work together like a team
Unite Black People
Build Black Self-Esteem

Unite Black People
All over the world today
Unite Black People
Empowered the united way

Unite Black People
Make it more than a dream
Unite Black People
A united Black Team!

The Toxic Brew

The twin evils
The two headed monster
Is killing Black People
In a day to day sequel

White supremacy
Is truly an enemy
And Black Self hate
We can't tolerate

They feed on
Each other
Killing off my
Sister and brother

The twin evils and
The lack of love of us
First kill off Black Self Hate
And watch White Supremacy evaporate

We can slay
The toxic brew
Black Self love
Will take us through

Or continue
Black Self Hate
Do what we got to do
Or die from the toxic brew

In Black Africa
Like South Africa
And the Congo
Let Self hate go

In African
America
From Chile
to Canada

We face the toxic brew
But we have the power
If we know what to do
Black Self Love for us me and you

End Black Self Hate
Watch white supremacy evaporate
End Black Self Hate
Watch White Supremacy evaporate

Reconciliation from Reparations

From the inside
Of my very soul
From the bones
Of my ancestors of old

Let our story
Be stated and told
Keep our people's love
Hot with passion not cold

Reconciliation
Through Reparations
Repair our soul
Include the young and old

Imagine peace
After atonement
For misdeeds of society
And the government

Imagine mass
Involvement
With a peace
That is heaven sent

That is the power
Of atonement
To cleanse the wrongs
Of society and government

From 3/5ths of Human
Taking names
Burning souls
And bones in flames

Lynching us
Stealing our inventions
Plotting and grabbing the land
Of the African

Reparations
Then reconciliation
Atonement from
Society and government

Dedicated to the crowd at the
Underground Poetry Series 1/19/08 event audience

Hopping

Like hipping
And hopping
There is no stopping
Black Love I'M dropping

Like music
That is popping
I love the flow
I'm dropping

Feeling our pain
Oppression is a stain
Another brother's blood
Washed down the drain

And the love
We should be
Sharing with
Love and caring

The madness
Must stop
Or see another
Brother drop

Stop the self-hating
And may be some gangster faking
Black Self Love
No faking

We are
Awakening
They are
Shaking

Self-hating faking
Hip hop Awakening
Open our eyes
So we can rise

Universal Black Love

Universal
Black Love
Throughout
The globe

Universal Black Love Mode
All around the globe
Universal Black Love
Must be our code

Brothers and sisters
Rejoin the fold
Universal Black Love
Let our story be told

Universal Black Love
Let our sun shine
Universal Black Love
In this our time

African-Americans and Africans
In America Africa, and Europe
Afro Canada, Caribbean and South Africa
Black Asia and Black Pacifica

Love in our
Relationships
Love is the focus
Of our video clips

Universal Black Love
Brothers and Sisters
Love our selves first
And then maybe we can love others

Universal; Black love
For Africa and the African
World Universal Black Love
Every Black man, woman boy and girl

Universal; Black Love
All over the African Globe
Universal Black Love
Must be our Universal Code

We Should Be Thinking Of

Let's bring back
One love
What else should we
Be thinking of

We die when
We spill our Blood
Show we from
The good black mud

Just because A brother
give you the eye
Settle it or let it go
Before both die

What else should?
We be thinking of
Brothers we need
One Love

Pressed up
Against the wall
United we stand
Divided we fall

About time we
Hear the calls
If we don't
Another Brother falls

Hold on too
Our common sense
Brothers now
Are way too tense

We all got to
Cool it down
Or many of us
Won't be around

Unite brothers
All over town,
Our sisters will
Lose their frown

What else should?
We be thinking of
Bring back
One Love

Chocolate Kiss

I love
To love you
My Black Woman
Speaking for the Black Man

We dance
We Live
Growing from the
love we give

I love your mind
I love your wit
If you ask me
I'm wit it

I love your curves
Your pretty eyes
I love your hips
And your pretty thighs

May our chocolate kiss
Last and last
May we love in the future
Like we loved in times past

You know we
brothers need you
And you should know
This is how I flow

Grow our love
Slow not fast
Make our chocolate love
Last and last

Love each other
Let us keep it together
Always remember
We are sister and brother

Give our love
With out a mask
So our chocolate kiss
Will last and last

We dance
We live
Surviving and growing
From the love we give

Love your soulful walk
Love your pillow talk
You are my sweetest thought
The one I have always sought

Love your wink
From your eye
Love it when
You say hi!

Love the way
We carry on
Sharing my love
In this song I mean Poem

May our sweet
chocolate kiss last and last
May we love each other in this time
Like we loved in the best of times past

CHOCOLATE LOVE

Explore chocolate love
As it is you see
And the strong bond
Chocolate love can be

Masculine
Tenderness
Feminine
Sweetness

Thick and Deep
Rich Chocolate
Considerate
Durable and delicate

A voluntary
Commitment
To promote
Mutual fulfillment

Love from
the tip
Chocolate Love
In the mind and grip

Chocolate Love
With potential
Chocolate Content
With love and commitment

Chocolate
Excitement

Emerging from
The love commitment

When Chocolate
Is love's glue!
And the rhythm
Of love that's true

When the love
Is shared by two
With real sensitivity
In love and unity

Two chocolate minds/bodies
Love is the remedy
Chocolate Togetherness
Love and happiness

We give love
To each other
The chocolate Love
We share together

Chocolate Love
Love and commitment
Chocolate Love
Is heaven sent

Chocolate Love
In many a shade
Chocolate Love
A loving colorful cascade

When We Come Together

It is a
Positive vibe
Greet your family and friends
Among the tribe

African-American History Month
Or any old time
Brothers' it's understood
The sisters are fine

From the East
And the West
When we are
At our very best

During KWANZAA or
at this festival
Where we share
Our story of survival

And share concerns
And share one love
And share our passion
Unite or plan a action

When we come together
As sister and Brother
We can respect and even
cherish each other

And welcome
Any other
To share it
Together

To Congratulate
Barack Obama
As President
Is time well spent!

African-American History
Month Share the joy in 09
With brothers who are good
And sisters who are smart, beautiful and very fine

When we come together
Like sister and brother
Share our joy
With any other

From the North
And the South
When we come together
As sister and Brother

When we share
The truth
With children
And youth

About life in Africa
Black inventions and slavery
Point to our future and
Salute our ancestors and our history

When we
Come together
My Sister and
My Brother

When We!!!

Grow Black Love

Wherever you are
Beautiful and strong Black Star
Near the coast
Or inland far

Like a beautiful
Black Dove
We must
Grow Black Love

The power of unity
To escape poverty
To combat police brutality
To attain true liberty

Grow Black Love
Don't push each other or shove
Hear a voice from above
Grow Black Love

Like a beautiful black rose
Like a beautiful Black dove
My people get it together
Grow Black on Black Love

Like smooth Black silk
Like strong Black Milk
Let us love each other
Be so united my sister and brother

Take off the
Fighting glove
Unite And
Grow Black Love

Don't push don't shove
Find Black unity/Black Love
Hear what I speak of
Grow Black Love

Grow Black Love
With your kin
Grow Black Love
With your friend

Grow black love
With your Black Rival
Grow Black Love
My People for Black Survival

Grow Black Love
Improve Black Friendships
Grow Black Love
And better Black Relationships

Grow Black Love
And better Black Marriages
Grow Black Love
And children in carriages

Grow Black Love
In our Ghetto
And our Black Community
You me and we!

Yours

Yours is the
Prettiest skin
You are my
Best friend

I love
The Skin
You
Are in

Yours is
The prettiest skin
We are kith and
Can be kin

Where you
Are thick or thin
Ours is Phat
Best friend! I love
The shape you in

Beauty is
Only skin deep
But your Love
Is so steep

Yours is the
Prettiest skin
The real thing love
My love and passion

The highest form of love
If we make it
What love is made of—
The real thing love

I love where you are thick
And where you thin
Because you are
my best friend

Tupoc And Biggie Small

We lost Tupoc
And Biggie Small
United We Stand
Divided we fall

Tis a shame
We ignore the call
United We Stand
Divided we fall

When a brother says
Up against the wall
United we stand
Divided we fall

We killed a
brother named Ron
And another named Paul
Some can't hear
The call at all

Shoot a brother
With a fire ball
United we stand
Divided we fall

Open your ears
Hear this call
United we stand
Divided we fall

We can be
Standing tall
United we stand
Divided We Fall

No mean mugging at
school or the mall
United We Stand
Divided we fall

We lost Tupoc
and Biggie Small
United We Stand
Divided We Fall

These two brothers died in unrelated circumstances but were at their strongest when they collaborated working together!

Maximum Respect

End deadly conflict
Among brothers and sisters
Always project
Maximum respect

Our survival
Must be our priority
Our unity in our
Community is the key

Oh what a better day
When peace and love we expect
A more-better world
Practicing maximum respect

Black on Black
Killing we must reject
Black Destiny
We must respect

Work together
Til we all are strong
Help each other
My sister and Brother

We must end
Violence among us
Then the others will
Give more respect to us

For our African essence
In the name of commonsense
Share maximum respect
Don't be on the fence

Keep cool runnings cool
Don't be a self-destruction tool
Show respect to sisters and brothers
Practice mutual maximum respect with others

Self-destruction
We must reject
Brothers and sisters always project
Maximum respect

The Sweetness of A Woman

The Sweetness
Of a woman
Is a phenomenon
That I can expand on

Yet there's more\
To learn
And real love
We earn

When she feels it
You will know it
If you blow it
She will show it

Visit her where]
She keeps her softness\
Love a woman
And feel her happiness

And if you try
Your very best
It is likely
You will see success

Win our best
Our championships
Join our sister
In great relationships

Enjoy a woman
Try to have fun
You will love
What you have done

Tough men
Are sensitive
Make sure Love
is what you give

Make sure love
is understood
Love a woman
Love her good

The sweetness
of a woman
Is a phenomenon
I can expand on

The Exceptional Black Woman

What is an
Exceptional Black Woman
She could be short
or tall, large or small!

Like Congress lady Barbara Lee
Or even Congress lady McKinney
Or Maxine Waters of LA known Locally,
nationally or internationally

They run corporations, countries
And households
Yet still they appreciate
A beautiful red rose

They discuss ideas
Not people
Young girls prepare
To be their equal

They are Black Women
With a major endeavor
They are Black Women
Who are very clever!

From very little
Great efforts have gone far
They shine like
A beautiful Black star

Exceptional Harriet Tubman
And Exceptional Queen Nzinga
Of Angola
Do you know her?

Without the
Exceptional Black Woman
Barren would be the fate
Of man and the land!

End Domestic Violence

In our lives
And in this building
I hope we men
Can share this feeling

From the floor
To the ceiling
Respect all women
Stop man-to-man killing

End partner homicide
So we can live with pride
End domestic violence
It's never justified

Practice mutual respect
Our sisters we must protect
Cause we can talk it out
We don't even have to shout

Mutual Respect we need
Together we grow a seed
Our children we must feed
Don't make a sister bleed

In our lives
We are building
Can we share?
This positive feeling

Don't hit
Scratch or shake
It is our progress
We must make

In this time
Push this hard-line
Violence we must end it
For the next level tip

In our lives
In every building
I hope we men
Can share this feeling

American Challenges in the Obama Era

American Challenges In the Obama Era

The November 2008 election of Barack Obama turned out to be one of the most important elections in American History and even African as well as African-American History. The devastation of the poor and middle classes of all communities under George Bush-2000 to 2008 made the November 08 election more important. And George Bush fed the rich with unprecedented tax cuts and fed the corporations like Halliburton with no bid contractor. The Oil Industry was given a free ride and so too were the banks and finance companies with their junk bonds. And with 2 unnecessary wars the arms industry was given more cash than they could possibly need from the overburdened taxpayers. And those 2 Bush wars were in the Middle East made hotter buy a lopsided Middle East Policy that spoke to a free Palestinian State but never produced a Palestinian State.

The Democrats began the election campaign with 6 or7 candidates but it soon became obvious that Barack Obama and Hillary Clinton were the front- runners. While the Republicans also had many candidates John McCain, Hugabee and Romny were the front-runners.

Again it must be said that Bush devastated the poor and middle classes purposely because he was a candidate of the rich and powerful classes as well as the far right and hard right neocons and conservatives. Progress made by African-Americans after 8 years of Bill Clinton 1992-2000 dissolved under the heel of the aristocratic George Bush 2000-2009.And we also witnessed the oppressive California 3 strike laws that imprisoned a greater percentage of African-Americans and other minorities mainly Mexicans than any other time since the days of slavery.

Although Hillary Clinton was favored to win over Barack Obama during the Democratic primaries initially because in America at that time it could be assumed that the white person naturally had the upper hand. But that was before the Obama era. And lest we for get that the African-American is a minority in America. However Obama finally won the nomination over Hillary winning mostly white populated states and diverse states too. Hillary remained gracious throughout but her husband Bill Clinton the former president did the heavy lifting for his wife and lost a lot of his popularity among some African-Americans.

John McCain prevailed among the so-called repugnant Republicans over Romny and Hugabee. John was well into his 70's causing many to think that he might not survive a 4-year presidential term due to the rigors of the office. As Barack Obama and John McCain began to campaign for the presidency in September and October of 2008, Obama received a present of sorts from the reckless disregard of George Bush in who had forgotten the Clitonian Monologue It's the economy stupid. Bush had deregulated all of his friends in the Banking and financial sector on wall street that many of them went crazy with the junk bonds and sub-prime housing loans and there was a shaky near financial meltdown with republican hands allover it. This factor helped to swing the momentum over to Obama and the democrats. Imagine that the American economy began to fall right in the heat of the presidential campaign with worthless unregulated junk bonds, massive housing foreclosures, financial bankruptcies by General Motors and Chrysler and many financial houses on Wall Street. Most of these Corporate and business interests and entities were in bed with the Bush Administration and the republicans suddenly giving the momentum to Barack Obama and the democrats.

Soon after the near collapse of the US Economy, Barack Obama won the US presidential election and began preparing to stand up a government and moved his family into the White House ironically built by African-American slaves.

Have no doubt about it Obama won but he did not get a full majority of the white voters to vote for him. Instead Obama got 92% of African-American votes and a huge majority of all of the immigrant and non-white voting populations while splitting the white vote with John McCain. No matter how he won Obama seams to be focused on being the President of all of America! And Barack Obama has become the first African-American President as well as becoming one of the most educated presidents in the history of the United States of America. After the primaries Obama made up with the Clintons and they assisted his efforts to win in every way they could causing a lot of women to vote for Obama from the Hillary Clinton camp.

So the central questions now becomes and is can America accept an African-American President? The world is watching the so-called oldest democracy! This challenge is profound and of fundamental propositions because of the history of racism in America from the first settlements, the slaughter of the Native Americans and the enslavement of African slaves brought from Africa to build the country with free labor, enslaved labor.

I had once outlined a book I never wrote about Kwame an African-American boy who grew up to be the first African-American president in 2048AD. Even I could not have predicted that America would elect a Black president during a time when African-Americans were wrongly marginalized and oppressed by George Bush and the republicans.

The census shift had informed my thought that by 2048 there would be a new majority of non-whites with some progressive whites and that a new majority party would emerge from the shambles of the present democratic party under the weight of anew majority in the US.

The Tea Baggers, Tea Party and Birthers movements have combined to form the we don't accept Barack Obama movement staining the acceptance of the majority of the US population that has accepted the new black president some ever so cautiously and some ever so critically. The most prominent and high placed Tea Party leader is Sarah Palin; John McCain's vice presidential pick and running mate. Sarah has tried to position herself to be the front-runner of the republican presidential candidate pool in 29012. However by aligning herself with the Birthers-a group of rightwing nuts who claim Obama was born in some other country with no proof what so ever when the man was born in Hawaii. These same rightwing nuts make no case against McCain who was born actually in Panama because well maybe because he is a White American. And with Sarah Palin aligning herself with the Birthers and the Tea Baggers she takes herself way out of the American political mainstream. These Tea Baggers spat on US Congressman and Civil Rights hero John Lewis and carried placards at their rallies with Obama painted as the joker a Batman cartoon character and Hitler, the German mass murderer. With friends like these Plain's strongest support will come from Ku Klux Klan types and a variety of the diehard racists. Although she will get some republican women's support she will be along shot to get the chance to run when she claims she can see Russia from her home in Wasilla, Alaska.

The republicans many of them like Russ Limbaugh and the rest of the right wing nuts have not yet accepted or come to terms with the fact that Barack Obama is the legitimately elected president of the USA. You see the Sarah Palin and Russ Limbaugh have never denounced the Birthers or the Tea Party republicans for mischaracterizations of Obama as Hitler or even the crowd that spat on John Lewis.

OBAMA LEGISLATIVE VICTORIES 2009-2010

Barack Obama has won a string of impressive legislative victories. The first victory was the 787 Billion dollar Stimulus1 to revitalize the nearly collapsed US Economy. These stimulus funds were passed in 2009 but are still working to provide jobs and critical support to states. The original Obama stimulus was even larger but was paired down by a not as bold Congress. Obama also used the TARP funding from the Bush Administration era to shore up some banks, and corporations like GM and Chrysler. Many banks failed during that time 2008-2009. Thanks to the Obama loans GM and Chrysler as well as many of the too big to fail banks have rebounded from near collapse however

Obama supporters have not yet recovered or benefited like the banks and corporations from the near total economic collapse that brought down the Bush Administration and the republicans.

Despite the stimulus1 funds have not been totally spent yet it is obvious tome that a stimulus ll is required and needed to rescue the American people in the inner cities and rural areas. And there some young people who have not had an opportunity to work or need a half way step from joblessness to having a job like a job boot camp or Adult Job Corps outlined earlier in my stimulus ll proposal earlier. As we approach the fall elections in early July here today it is my profound hope that Obama will quickly embrace the need for Stimulus ll to make away for supporting the young unemployed form all over America who supported his candidacy. The republicans are hoping he will not embrace a stimulus ll so they can derive a wedge between Obama and his millions of unemployed or underemployed supporters this fall! Or see these you voters of every ethnic and color stay away from the polls because they are not employed or hopelessly discouraged..

The biggest victory by far has been the Healthcare reform followed by the recent financial and banking reforms recently passed, But now there needs to be a comprehensive jobs bill or stimulus ll put on the table to energize young Obama supporters prior to the 2010 elections or a disaster could occur.

The Oil Spill In the Gulf

We all remember hearing Sarah Palin shout drill Baby Drill during the November 2008 Presidential election. But now we are 65 days into the most horrible oil spill in the history of oil drilling in the US at least since the Valdez in Alaska. Daily these days we see gallons and an unknown number of barrels of oil spilling in to the Gulf of Mexico affecting Louisiana, Mississippi, and Florida Coastline. The Oil Spill has challenged Obama because there are no easy answers and historically the federal government has depended on the Oil Industry to prepare for emergencies and respond to these types of emergencies based on their emergency plans submitted when the license to drill has been granted. Apparently the Bush Administration was so much in bed with the oil industry that they allowed oil companies to write their own safety plans and reports. Now it is obvious that Shell BP had no plan to shutoff the oil after11 people died after the platform blew up in the gulf. This oil spill has challenged Obama as well as the republicans who want to cut the size of the American government even more when the government needs to have the power to respond to a disaster of this magnitude especially when the corporations fail like Shell BP failed to respond appropriately in the Gulf.

The Biggest American Challenges

The biggest American challenges for President Obama and America after a proper amount of acceptance is ending 2 Bush initiated wars as soon as possible in Iraq and Afghanistan while somehow establishing a viable connected Palestinian State. Ending of inner-city unemployment is the root cause of the disproportionately high rate of inner-city youth and presents a substantial challenge for all of America in 2010.Obama will do well to remember as Bill Clinton once said, "It's The Economy Stupid". Now more than ever it is the economy President Obama!

If you go to YouTube and type in the Nigerian Oil Spills in the Nigerian Delta, you will see that Shell BP and Standard Oil have created a similar disaster to the Gulf Oil Spill now impacting Texas as well as the other3 American Gulf states. The oil spill damages in the Gulf of Mexico and the Nigerian Delta are gigantic challenges for America, Africa and the world spotlighting oil companies guilty as sin. The clean up of these oil-producing areas constitute a gigantic ecological challenge for America, Africa and the world. President Obama Smartly sought and received a 20 Billion dollar clean up and rescue fund – a great move from Shell British Petroleum but will it be enough?

President Barack Obama has his challenges in the Gulf of Mexico, the Middle East, and the American inner cities as well as in shutting down 2 unwise, unpopular wars! Then there is the challenge of the 2010 Congressional elections faced by President Obama. Still America has a continuing challenge to accept its first African-American President.

And African-Americans have a gigantic challenge to seek employment for its millions of underemployed, unemployed people. Additionally with 70% of African- American marriage aged women unable or in some cases unwilling to marry places a challenge on African-American men and women to rescue the dieing Black family/Black Romance/Black Love/African American Ethnic glue and the efforts must be made up by Black men and Black women.

The killing of Inner City Blacks in an unjustifiable manner like the killing Mathew Johnson in San Francisco's Hunters Point in 1967 (that sparked the 1967 Hunters Point Riot/rebellion) to Larry Lumpkin in San Francisco's in Lakeview area May 20, 1986, The murder of Sean Bell in New Your City a night before his wedding with 50 bullets fired into and a young unarmed African-American or how can we in San Francisco for get the SFPD outright and unjustified killing of Cameron Boyd in 2004 or the killing of young African-American men all over the USA by armed police is one of the gravest and deadliest challenges faced not only by African-Americans, it is a challenge for everyone who lives in America because each of the occurrences of this type of deadly police brutality sprays vomit all over the US constitution, flag and way of life. This is a vomit of filth, racial injustice and oppressive stain that will not wipe clean as long as it continues to occur like it did in an Oakland, CA at the Fruitvale Bay Area Rapid Transit Station as the young father—Oscar Grant as he laid face down on the ground and was assassinated by Johannes Mehserle a BART policeman recently on a New Years Eve 2009. The trial is now in the jury deliberation stage with an all white jury but many times like with Larry Lumpkin murdered by the soldiers of the state- SFPD despite protests there is no trial and the beat goes on!

Equally hideous and ignorant is the Black on Black violence among Africa- Americans, and the Brown on Brown violence of our Latinos/Latinas although the high unemployment rate and high incarceration rate feds these negative impulses/situations and competition for slim resources underlay this type of ethnic or internal violence that is suicidal and leaves too many widows and fatherless and even motherless children.

We cannot allow this genocidal violence internally among ourselves or externally by rogue and lawless police in our communities to continue as we too many times see it occur. These are gigantic challenges that we must face and make sure stop occurring.

Africa must challenge itself by abandoning the failed mini-states and forging a gigantic Continent wide country and government to make by any name to make Africans all over the world proud of our African roots and to make Africa's teaming young millions have a stake in building up an egalitarian society strong enough to feed, clothe and otherwise take care of itself independently with all of it's vast resources or remain a dependent but totally rich continent. Africa too has it's challenges and President Obama should also use his power of thought to discuss the formation of a United States of Africa concept with every African President and Ambassador he meets with but the development of a Federated States of Africa or African Peoples Republic must come to the continent of Africa from the ground up making Africa and African's challenge a substantial challenge but currently requires thinking out of the box to truly ever become the reality that will help Africa and Africans develop to their full potential for the benefit of Africa's people instead of delivering unending profits to multinational corporations that have emerged and evolved to play the same sinister roles played in the past by the colonial powers.

The last of America's greatest challenges is to find a way to treat 12 to 20 million immigrants mostly from Mexico but also South and Central America as well as Africa and the Caribbean Islands some who are here illegally with dignity and compassion like each American would like their family treated while in the land of others. Deporting 12 to 20 million people would be a messy disaster that would make America look like the old racist 1993 Apartheid South Africa. Thinking out the box says maybe close all borders North and South then once the borders are completely sealed then give all immigrants currently here a blanket amnesty and paths to citizenship! However as long as US soldiers are stretched all over the world in over 600 military bases there will never be enough soldiers to seal the US Borders. Deporting 12 to 20 million people is too much like the American system of slavery or Nazi Germany in these modern times by the so-called leading democracy and already we see that deporting people like it is happening today involves separating families like slavery with the children being born in America and citizens while their parents are deported never possibly never to see their children and families again. America has to rethink this whole issue on a humanitarian basis and reject the savage ways of the past and present to enjoy a prosperous and united future.

The challenges of the world facing America and President Barack Obama are vast and even daunting. One could even say the challenges of the world today are overwhelming. So thinking out of the box or new thinking must be encouraged so that creative and humanitarian solutions can be arrived at that will leave this country in a better position to lead the world by example and not by ways that leave the rest of the world calling the USA the greatest hypocrites in the world. These are the dynamic challenges faced by President Obama and America and I humbly challenge America and President to get out of the box of past and present thinking and explore new thinking to resolve the challenges faced by America and Americans of every type and President Barrack Hussein Obama.

Postscript:

The verdict is now in and the jury of mostly white jury with a 3 Hispanics compromised and did not even convict Johannes Mehserle with first degree or second decree murder—The judge took those charges off the table making the trial a whitewash. The jury completed the whitewash by refusing to convict Mehserle with Manslaughter or even voluntary manslaughter but compromised on the slap on the wrist involuntary manslaughter charge. Still Mehserle faces up to14 years in prison and Oakland erupted in protests downtown and 100 or more were arrested that night while a Footlocker Store was looted and gutted by multiracial protesters. The next episode will occur when the sentencing of Mehserle who allegedly called his victim a bitch ass N----- while he lay down facing the cold ground cuffed an alive facedown Oscar Grant was assassinated and handcuffed Grant after assassinating him. I feel this was a hate crime. These are the challenges faced by America and President Barack Obama in 2010.